RITTER IN RESIDENCE

Ritter

A Comic Collection by

in Residence

Erika Ritter

A DOUGLAS GIBSON BOOK

M&S

Canadian Cataloguing in Publication Data

Ritter, Erika, date
Ritter in residence

ISBN 0-7710-7530-8

I. Title

PS8585.I88R5 1987   C818'.5407   C87-094319-7
PR9199.3.R587R5 1987

Printed and bound in Canada by John Deyell Co.

A Douglas Gibson Book

McClelland and Stewart
The Canadian Publishers
481 University Avenue
Toronto M5G 2E9

To my irreplaceable friends,
who find me funny especially when I'm not,
and who take me seriously
especially when I don't deserve it,
this book is disrespectfully dedicated,
with genuine love and gratitude.

Contents

Preface

In case you're concerned about it, let me assure you that there's a lot more behind the title *Ritter in Residence* than an irresistible urge to make a pun coupled with the overwhelming need to work the author's name in somehow.

Like many other writers in this country, I have done time in federal and provincial institutions of writerly residence. I have paid rent to the university for the use of an elderly manual typewriter with a sticking "s"; I have performed vocal warm-ups with actors at venerable Canadian theatrical facilities, in order to demonstrate that a playwright in residence is capable of tangible accomplishment. I have even lined up for cold cereal and cream in the company of the tousled morning faces of the students at a venerable American women's college, marvelling at the vulnerability of the outsized bunny slippers peering from beneath the hems of their sprigged nightgowns, at the same time as I stood in awe of the cool sophistication with which they flipped through *The Boston Globe* over coffee and cigarettes.

Best of all, I have forged warm and enduring friendships in even the unlikeliest of these circumstances, which have served to reassure me, later on, that I didn't in fact just dream these assignments up.

Although, on balance, these experiences have been enjoyable, I have also learned that being a writer in residence means, above all, abiding by the contradiction inherent in the very job description. For, by definition, a writer is an outsider, the person alone, someone never quite at home in the world upon which he comments. A writer comfortably in residence, therefore, wouldn't really be a writer at all – which condemns writers always to find ways of making themselves uncomfortable in their literary domains, just to keep the output flowing.

Certainly, a Ritter cosily ensconced in residence is no more imaginable a concept than a writer in residence, as this batch of essays readily indicates. The world, to me, is always a little out of whack, and full of things that don't stand up, somehow, under scrutiny. Luckily, though, the process of blowing life as we know it out of the water is an essentially light-hearted one for me, and I hope the results are enjoyable to you.

But if not, I don't see, offhand, how you can come and complain to me about it. Those of us not quite at home in the world don't quite have permanent addresses either.

ERIKA RITTER
In Residence, But Not
Entirely at Home
July 1987

Scotch Ads
on the Rocks

For me, one of the highlights of a generally undistinguished childhood was reading the series of ads for Canadian Club whiskey that appeared in most magazines.

I'm sure you remember those ads. A snapshot-illustrated narrative would tell the story of a young man and his blonde companion (although sometimes several young-and-blonde couples underwent the ordeal together) who got caught up in an open-air adventure in some exotic land.

"When they told us we hadn't experienced the Amazon until we'd wrestled alligators," the tale would typically begin, "we thought they were joking. But the joke – and ultimately the alligators – were on us."

It wasn't always alligators, of course. Sometimes this

game-and-suggestible young couple got to endure a few menacing moments with the Mudmen of New Guinea, or shared some sherbet with the Sherpas, or tobogganed down a set of Madagascar rapids clinging to a large jungle leaf. Whatever the escapade, though, the upshot was always the same. As well as the snapshot. The g-and-s young couple and a few friends relaxing in some exotic bar where, as the caption inevitably declared, "we toasted our adventure with Canadian Club, the Best in the House in 87 Lands."

As an impressionable child, I came to believe those ads foretold what adult life was going to be like. Alligators and Mudmen lay ahead to be dealt with – just like the mortgage payments and the job interviews that the grown-ups of my closer acquaintance used as rationales for having a drink. And if I wondered exactly *whom* I was going to share my Canadian Club adventures with, the answer was provided by *another* ad campaign of the time, this one for Dewar's Scotch.

The Dewar's Profile featured the kind of guy who'd be up for anything, be it Mudman or mortgage payment. Sometimes he was an author, sometimes a businessman. Eventually, as human history progressed to a plateau of higher enlightenment, he might even yield his place to a lady physicist or a female balloonist. But whoever the subject of the Profile was, like the Canadian Club couple, he or she gave the promise that adulthood was going to entail lots of whiskey and derring-do.

That's why it strikes me as a particularly embarrassing anachronism that the Dewar's people have resurrected the Profile campaign, and are once again attempting to make an equation between grown-up adventures and grown-up drinks. Just whom do they think they're kidding? Because now, you see, I'm an adult myself and know that whiskey-drinkers simply aren't like that.

Take the Profile guy they ran in a recent ad. His name is Alistair Ballantine, but if he feels any brand-name confusion about pitching a Scotch called Dewar's, his clear-eyed gaze doesn't show it. Nor does the huge elephant (no, seriously) hulking nearby appear to be any cause for discomfiture.

Because Alistair is president of a safari company by Profession, and his Hobby, wouldn't you know it, is playing elephant polo in Nepal. His Last Book Read was by Graham Greene, and the Quote from his no-nonsense lips is, "Boredom is perhaps the one thing everybody can do well without."

Well, gosh. I don't buy it for a second, do you? I mean, there's old Alistair with his trusty elephant over his shoulder, his elephant polo mallet idling in his hands, and a chapter of Graham Greene to look forward to before he turns in. . . . What does this man know about boredom? And if he's having as much fun as he claims, what on earth does he require from Scotch? Surely all he needs to round out an already full and dehydrating day is a thermos-capful of Gatorade.

No, if the Dewar's people are sincerely interested in pitching their product to today's cynical and incredulous adult, they should hand Alistair his pink slip, and give over the Profile duties to someone far more representative of our times. To someone like . . . well, not to get pushy about it, but . . . to someone more like *me*.

Now, before you dismiss the idea out of hand, let me sketch out my Profile, to give you a better idea of what I mean:

ERIKA RITTER. *Home*: The place where the bank sends the overdraft statement. *Age*: Old enough to know how to duck the question. *Profession*: Gentle self-mockery. *Hobby*: Making up plausible-sounding activities so that my résumé will give the illusion of good social adjustment. *Last Book Read*: As much of Alice Munro's latest as I could, before the sales staff at Coles' started giving me dirty looks. *Latest Accomplishment*: Getting through the entire This Week's Bestsellers list without once having to make an actual consumer purchase. *Why I Do What I Do*: More my therapist's problem than mine, really, if you ask me. *Quote*: "I'll have a Dewar's, I guess – or, wait a sec. What's your cheapest bar Scotch?"

You see? The Profile of the kind of person you can really *accept* as someone who deserves a shot of Scotch. And a far more plausible symbol of late-twentieth-century adulthood than any safari captain or lady parachutist could ever be.

Well, anyway, while you're thinking it over, I'm going to send my proposal along to the Dewar's people. Besides, even if they don't go for it, there's always the gang at Canadian Club. I'm planning to suggest they revive the Canadian Club adventure idea, reconstructed around me. "When they proposed braving the discount food terminal at five to six on the brink of a holiday weekend, I thought they had to be kidding. . . . "

Oh, you kid

I'll bet you a Fisher-Price Activity Centre to a Sesame Street bib covered in spit-up that all of your friends have babies now. In fact, if you're like me, most of your friends are now well into their second baby, which means they clearly intend to make more than a passing fad out of this parenting thing.

Which means, in turn, that you will be forced to take seriously your role as Friend of the Family, and learn to deal with your friends' babies as permanent facts of *your* life, too.

All of this by way of lead-up to the inevitable announcement that I am in the process of attempting to produce yet another how-to book, and plan to try out the first few chapter proposals on you.

Chapter One: *Naming the Baby*. The best advice I can offer in this area is *Don't*. Although the very pregnant couple masquerading as your best friends in all the world will importune you for input on this important subject, the truth of the matter is that tastes and trends change so rapidly in this area that there is virtually no chance of your landing on the money in your choice of a name.

For instance, back when twenties nostalgia was in vogue, it was fashionable to christen girls as if they were Hemingway heroines, with names like Brett and Jordan. Boys of that era got to be Brett and Jordan too, unless their parents opted for more manly monikers like Jake and Cal. Small wonder, really, that the children of that epoch of American literary inspiration have never progressed beyond monosyllabic discourse, circumspect mistrust of the opposite sex, and a morbid fear of rain that they might end up dead in.

Similarly, biblically prompted handles like Judah and Jeroboam are pretty passé now, sharing the Out List with those Masterpiece Theatre Names straight out of Trollope and Austen. So popular were Masterpiece Theatre names in their day, though, that the day-care centres of this country are now awash with small sober individuals called Emma and Nicholas – and woe betide you if you down-size the name to fit the tot by abbreviating it to Emmy or Nick.

And don't expect to find favour with your newly babied friends by proposing a corporate-merger name like Harris or Whitney, either. Although liberally doled out to infants in the late seventies, capitalistic nomenclature has gone the way of what I like to think of as the Paper Product Names from the fifties – namely, Kimberly if you're a girl, and for a boy, Scott.

So what *is* in, in the name-game right now? Surprisingly, the dullest of the dull, names like Howard and Myrna and Edith and Fred that belonged to great-aunts and -uncles. Either those, or appellations of bizarre origin, such as Ruka, Chino, or Gahereth – obviously created by selecting Scrabble tiles randomly from a hat.

Chapter Two: *Gifting the Baby Who Has Everything*. Having adroitly sidestepped the deadfall of suggesting names for the child, do not stumble blindly into the quick-lime pit of selecting the wrong gift for young Howard or Ruka.

Remember always that it's not the child you're impressing here, it's the parents, and make your purchase accordingly. For example, a plastic crib mobile makes a good gift only if you don't mind seeing your paltry present overshadowed by the Calder installation or the Wieland wall-hanging more discerning friends have proffered.

Best to go with a smartly sloganed T-shirt for the tyke, on condition that you choose an ideologically correct caption like "Member of the Laleche Little League", or "My Playpen Is a Nuclear Weapons Free Zone".

If in doubt, however, my fail-safe advice is that you make your purchase at some trendily over-priced kids' shoppe with a name like La Grenouille Méchante, so that if the T-shirt itself finds no favour, the kid can always wear the designer bag it came in.

Of course, there is always the craven alternative of buying a present for the parents instead, but even there, success is by no means automatic. Those light-hearted sweatshirts from non-critical years past, with "Myrna's Mother" and "Gahereth's Dad" on them, are now simply too banal to inspire more than a polite yawn.

Additionally, you are wise to stay away from anything in the guide-to-baby-care line of books, for the very simple reason that those earnest souls who used to be your friends have already bought the store out of every conceivable title, conceivably before the child was even conceived. So you can rest assured that any volume they don't have, they don't *want*, which is why you are well advised to steer clear of titles like the following: *Why Infants Have No Aptitude for French*; *Coping with the Ordinary Child*; *Why Single Friends Don't Wish to Discuss Day Care*; or *The Refreshing Lack of Meaning in Children's Artwork*.

Chapter Three: *Playing Your Part*. The role of the childless friend of the family is not to extol the joys of independence, or to betray for one single second that, truth be told, you're just as happy that the patter of little feet around *your* house originates with the racoons in the attic, and that you have nothing in the oven except a single serving of zucchini lasagna from Lean Cuisine.

Your baby-encumbered friends don't need to hear things like that. What your baby-encumbered friends *do* need to hear is how sadly silent your place seems in contrast to the rollicking merriment of their populous hearth. They need you to beg them to make "Auntie" or "Uncle" the baby's first decipherable utterance, once he has his French irregular verbs down pat.

Above all, they need you to remind them of the more hellish aspects of the selfish, dead-ended, solipsistic, directionless, heedless, and childless life that drove them to take the parental plunge in the first place.

However, even with the best intentions in the world, it's not always possible to remember exactly how diplomatically your friends with babies have to be treated. After all, we're talking about a deprived demographic group, for whom the notion of an uninterrupted night's sleep rings with a resonance more exotic than the concept of interplanetary manned space travel.

These are people who no longer remember what it feels like to venture out-of-doors without first ramming the wildly flailing limbs of a screaming two-year-old into a snowsuit with jammed zippers, and then bumping a stroller with pathological wheel-lock down a set of broken apartment stairs. These are, in other words, people whose kid-ridden state underscores the fact that they must be treated with kid gloves. For that reason, a quick checklist of what and what not to say to these hair-trigger lunatics is not only advisable but essential.

Do Not Say:

"The day you were awarded that Rhodes Scholarship, did you ever imagine yourself knee-deep in soiled Pampers and tins of Simulac?"

"I guess when it's your *own* child crying, it doesn't drive you crazy in the same way, right?"

"Maybe you should have lined up a reliable baby-sitter before you got pregnant, huh?"

"The great thing is, I can enjoy him for an hour, and then hand him back to *you* when his diaper needs changing."

"Boy, that kid has really figured out how to pull *your* strings."

"I suppose there's no way of knowing beforehand what kind of disposition they'll have."

"Why don't you just take the kid down to his office and say, 'Hey, *you* look after her for a while'?"

"That's the problem, of course. Once you've got them, you can't send them back, ha, ha."

Do Say:

"But think of all the bad meals in expensive restaurants you're missing, and the boring parties and rotten films."

"Look at that smile. Doesn't it make it all worth while?"

"I figured a VCR would make a good baby-shower gift."

"I'd *love* to take him for the afternoon. People in the park will think he's mine."

"Yours is the only baby I've ever met who doesn't look like Truman Capote."

"You make it all look so easy."

"Up until now, I could have sworn I didn't want kids."

Chapter Four: *Some Basic Terminology*. Finally, no how-to guide is complete without a list of some of the more esssential words you're going to need if you expect to communicate with those baby-besotted strangers you used to think you knew.

OshKosh. The sound a small child makes when he or she sits down on your knee with a very full diaper.

Steiff. The period of rule in Germany that immediately preceded Hitler's rise to power. Not to be confused with the *Gund*, which was a cartel of German business interests that co-existed with the Steiff, at a point in history markedly more light-hearted than the atmosphere that informs your friends' home as they attempt to get the baby to take a nap.

Playschool. A contradiction in terms, as the name suggests. The effort involved in getting the child there, and the amount of money necessary to keep him there, both obviate any aspects of "play" for the parents, while "school" may be too august a term for a pile of recycled construction paper, a grubby Cookie Monster puppet, and a box of no-name arrowroot.

Au Pair. A mythological creature similar to the hypogriff, which dwells in exotic countries, is seldom seen, but is continually longed for, especially when all of the above have ceased to beguile the child.

Sharon, Lois, and Bram. A form of retributive justice that inevitably befalls those who used to dismiss Peter, Paul, and Mary as too simplistic.

Well, as usual, I haven't really thought out my how-to book completely, and the whole project threatens to die a-borning, so to speak, as so many of my best ideas do.

But I must be on the right track, because when I showed it to a friend of mine who is the mother of two children under the age of three, she said all that was missing was a chapter on a hundred and one ways to serve Alpha-Getti.

A
Renovated
Doll's House

At first, I couldn't believe who was sitting in the guest's chair on the Phil Donnybrook Show: Nora Helmer, the heroine of Ibsen's play *A Doll's House*. There she was, chatting cosily about what had been happening in her life since she slammed the door on her paternalistic husband, Torvald, back in 1879, and walked out into the Norwegian night to find herself.

"I've been through some changes, Phil," Nora was averring.

I'll say. Jauntily jumpsuited with a smart little haircut, she'd come miles from the crinolined central character of Ibsen's creaky old play, and looked terrific for a woman her age.

21

"You know, Phil, when I left Torvald and set out to earn my own living, I didn't have a bean. My God, I'd even left my wedding ring behind."

"I remember," Donnybrook nodded. "A gutsy move it was, for the time."

"Anyway, once I'd walked, the number one priority was money, and what did I know from the working world? Zilch. All I'd ever done as Torvald's wife was dance the tarantella at parties and wolf chocolate macaroons, right? So I took the only work I could find that seemed commensurate with my skills: I danced tarantella in a cheap club until the sexual harassment drove me out. Then I got a job in a chocolate-macaroon factory."

"And that's when the process of politicization really began for you."

"You bet, Phil. In fact, it was a happening time for women generally. In my first week on the line, I found that the guy packing chocolates next to me was earning twenty kroner a week more. By the next week I'd become one of a group of women who met regularly over cheap red wine and cheez-twists to discuss subsidized day care, male domination, and whatever else came up."

"The birth of modern feminism as we know it. . . . "

"Back then we didn't think of it as feminism, Phil. Just common sense. Anyway, soon we were publishing a magazine and picketing all the local beauty pageants. It was a hell of a lot of fun."

Nora paused to light up another Virginia Slim ("I'm still in the process of quitting, Phil") and expelled a thoughtful puff of smoke. "We made some real political gains for women, too – at least we thought we did.

"Within ten years I'd made it to second vice-president in charge of product improvement, where I completely turned the company's profit picture around with the sugar-free macaroon. Oh sure, my love life was the pits, thanks to I.F. – that's career-lady talk for Intimidation Factor. But I'd forged some real bonds with other women and had my priorities straight, and . . . "

As she paused, she looked more sober – and older. "And it was just about then that it all went wrong."

"Hold that thought, Nora. We'll be right back after a commercial break."

Following a cavalcade of ads, mostly offensive to women, Nora clarified what she meant by it all going wrong. "The inevitable conservative backlash. And I'm not talking about the Total Woman stuff. I mean within the women's movement itself, with some feminists finding themselves aligned with fundamentalist kooks on the pornography thing. And other liberated women joining high-powered clubs where the girls get to take steam and intimidate the coat-check gal in an elitist atmosphere, just like the boys.

"So lately, Phil, I'm wondering just how far I've really come. I mean, for instance, when my promotion to first vice-president resulted in rumours that my boss and I were having an affair – "

"Hey, but what a book you wrote about being fired, Nora! I couldn't put it down."

"Thanks, Phil. Sure, the book defrayed some of my legal costs, but the point is – "

"The point is, you've *survived*. And what the ladies out there in the audience would like to know is: How is tomorrow shaping up for Nora Helmer?"

Nora shrugged. "Well, I keep busy with my tarantella classes and public appearances. And of course, Torvald and I are talking to each other at last."

"No! You mean there might be a reconciliation in the wings for naturalistic theatre's favourite feuding couple?"

"I wouldn't go that far. But Torvald's been through some changes too, in the past hundred years or so. After he ran through a succession of young bimbos, there was a brief flirtation with homosexuality – "

"You're kidding!"

"Then there was a long period of complete sexual indifference. But now I think Torvald's really learning how to relate to women in an open, non-competitive way, and the last time we had lunch, he – "

"Glad to hear it, Nora, but I'm afraid we're just about out of time. Ladies, let's have a big hand for today's guest, Ms. Nora Helmer, the lead character from . . . "

As I turned off the set, Phil was in the process of telling us that tomorrow's special guest would be Robinson Crusoe, on hand to discuss time-share condos in the tropics.

Pondering the Imponderables

For years now Erika and the girls have been getting together over diet cola and sushi to debate some of the deeper mysteries of our age.

"Forget prospects for peace in the Middle East," says Sonya. "What I want to know is, how come I'm the only person I know whose eyeshadow always cakes into greasy little lines across my eyelids?"

"Good question," says Joanne. "But I've got some even better ones. Why does perfume last longer on other women than it does on me? And how did I get to be thirty-seven years old and *still* have no beauty routine? I'm still washing my face in ice-water every night because I once read that Paul Newman did that to keep his skin so tight. All that's happened to me over the years is that I'm starting to look more and more like Paul Newman. I swear, sometimes I feel as though every other woman came into the world equipped with a how-to manual that was never issued to me."

Right you are, Joanne. Sometimes I have that feeling too, although I like to flatter myself that my concerns run deeper than the merely cosmetic. Flirting is the big one. I mean, at least my friend Sonya knows how to bat her eyelids at some prospective romantic quarry, no matter how badly made-up they may be.

But luckily at this moment I am torn away from brooding contemplation of my life as the John Turner of sexual politics by a vivid cry of pain at my elbow from my friend Marina.

"That's not the worst," declares Marina. "I'll tell you what's the worst. It's that first dinner out with a new man. Who pays?"

A look of panic passes around the sushi table. Uh-oh. It was only a matter of time before someone brought this one up. And Marina is right. It is definitely the worst. Should you split the bill with him or shouldn't you?

"Five years ago," I sigh, "I would have said split it."

"Five years ago," Marina snaps back, "I would have picked up the entire tab just to prove to him I had nothing to prove. Now things seem to be going back the other way. After a few more readings of *The Total Woman*, I figure I'll be able to just sit there smiling a seraphic little Buddha smile while the bill lies on the table between us like an exhibit for the prosecution."

"Marina! That's so retrograde."

"What, I should go back to insisting that I pay for exactly half? That kind of militancy is pretty retrograde too."

Sonya ponders for a moment, then her face lights up with a eureka smile. "I've got it. The thing to do is *offer* to pay for your half. Very quickly, just once. You know, to show him you're willing to share the positive fall-out of feminism? Then you let him pick up the whole thing. To show him his manhood is not under assault."

Another exchange of looks as we try to determine whether to buy that idea, just for the sake of moving the conversation along. Personally, I'm prepared to buy it, because there is a much more burning issue I want to bring up: How come, in the movies, women can always whip their hair into a coil on top of their heads in about four seconds, fasten it with a single bobby pin, and it stays there for the rest of the picture? While in real life it would take two hours, a bottle of hairspray, and a riveting gun to get the same effect.

Hour by hour, deep into the night, the questions rage on, over plates smeared with soy sauce and the wilting remnants of raw-tuna-and-rice rolls that bear mute testimony to the compelling force of the need to talk combined with the irresistible urge of a big maki attack.

Why is it that Joanne's mother wore gloves and a smart little veil just to do the housework, while Joanne feels overdressed if her sweatpants match her top?

And what of Erika? How can she expect to find true happiness, when she has so far been unable even to find a way of laughing aloud that does not shatter glassware in neighbouring restaurants and startle the waiters like frightened deer?

Meanwhile, Sonya wants to know why she runs into sexually tempting men only when she has failed to shave her legs.

If only we knew, we lament to each other, like a bad road-company production of *The Three Sisters*. If only we knew.

Hats Off —

I Think

I have to state right off the bat that I have a certain amount of ambivalence about hats. What it comes down to is the fact that I like the *idea* of hats much better than I like the hats themselves. In that sense, hats are much like horses – delightful to contemplate in the abstract, but a little scary when you get up close.

I think you know what I mean. You're walking past a store window and there, on tempting display, is a smart-looking borsalino that promises, almost audibly, to change your life immediately and for the better.

If only I had that hat, you think to yourself, I could rule the world. Personality, rugged individualism, *savoir-faire* – all of these elusive qualitics sccm embodied by that borsalino, and nothing will do but that you buy it.

And so you do, and so your life *is* dramatically upgraded. For exactly six minutes. Which is precisely the length of time required to find out that your new hat is (a) uncomfortable, (b) unpopular in movie theatres, (c) treacherous on crowded buses, and (d) more aerodynamically apt than even *The Spirit of St. Louis* when it comes to taking off in a good tail wind.

At that point, with some embarrassment, you retrieve the borsalino from the gutter into which it's blown, brush off the brim, then quietly file the hat away on the top closet shelf, along with other evidence of ill-advised consumerist zeal, including those asymmetrical baskets from Chad that were going to make such ingenious Christmas gifts, and the green mohair coat you never got around to dyeing.

What went wrong with the concept of the hat? Time was, nobody would be seen outdoors without one. When office towers of the fifties spilled their grey-flannelled male inhabitants onto the pavement at five o'clock, the street became a river of bobbing fedoras and Homburgs. Women's hat-shops flourished on every corner, ready to cater to the generally held belief that there was very little that could go amiss in a miss's life that the acquisition of a new hat couldn't fix.

It's a particular tragedy of women, in fact, that they have found nothing in the eighties with which to replace the old notion of salvation through millinery. Wan efforts to cheer up are still sometimes made by going to the hairdresser, but the results there are no more satisfying than they ever were.

Of course, as technology becomes a more and more pervasive element of our lives, women are making a concerted stab at feeling better through personal computers, although some ineffable quality of frivolity is somehow missing in the attempt. Ditto to feeling better through corporate take-over, which, although all very well in its way, yields absolutely nothing that can be triumphantly borne off in a round striped box tied up with broad ribbon.

Funnily enough, men seem to be surviving the demise of the hat in a spirit of defiance that is as touching as it is inappropriate. You can witness this phenomenon for yourself any time you see a group of men gathered together for fun. Men who find their fun in politics (especially men who are losing their hair, which is so often a by-product of political involvement) often still wear little peaked caps or Che-style berets, or navy toques of a vaguely stevedorish sort. Meanwhile, men in the arts and academe try to strike a more flamboyant and evocative pose with Stetsons or deerstalkers or woven broad-brimmed hats similar to what the Impressionists wore.

In most cases, though, men in hats are to be avoided at all costs. In my experience, it is practically always men in hats who are liable to show you their first drafts at the drop of a you-know-what, lecture you on the fallacies inherent in supply-side economics, and talk so loudly in the elevator that you are reduced to pretending that this is some demented stranger who has followed you on board, instead of your husband of nineteen years.

No one can account for the unseemly behaviour of men with hats, unless it connects in some way to the more general phenomenon of people putting on hats when they wish to behave foolishly *en masse*. As at a company convention, or a New Year's Eve party, or when filing off a charter flight from a Caribbean holiday to greet the blizzard with predictable cries of woe and giant straw sombreros.

We can, however, say one thing with absolute certainty: As surely as the wearing of hats used to symbolize good social integration and an acceptance of the status quo, so today does the hat represent the complete opposite. A hat these days is a statement, a hat is an anachronism, a hat bespeaks defiance.

So far so good. Now, if only someone could get the hats away from the conventioneers, and find a way to anchor them in the wind . . . Why, I'd take my hat off to him.

Pet Teachers

I don't want to give you the erroneous impression that my childhood relationships with teachers were always harmonious. Back in Grade Five, for instance, we had a hideous young woman in dowdily pleated skirts and rimless glasses who made a special project of making my life hell, as she'd made hell of my brother's life before me. But perhaps my own particular set of problems with this malevolent soul can be dated from the day that, impatient to answer a question, I waved my arm vigorously in the air in the time-honoured manner of a student signalling eagerness to be called upon.

What I forgot was that the hand at the end of the waving arm had an uncapped fountain pen in it. Within a few moments, the most alarmingly inexplicable Peacock Blue flecks began to appear on the front of my teacher's white Ban-lon sweater set. Then on her pale perpetually unhappy-looking countenance, and finally on the lenses of her thick rimless glasses.

Even more astounding to report, the longer I continued to thrash my arm in the air seeking her attention, the thicker the spattering of blue spots upon her person.

Needless to say, it took my teacher less time than it took me to figure out the connection between my arm-waving and the freckling of ink on her front, and while I cannot recall my punishment for this unwitting infraction, it was no doubt swift and horrible – as you'd expect from a woman who could fasten shut the mouth of a talker with Scotch tape, compel a gum-chewer to wear the detected wad on the end of her nose, or lock a child who'd neglected his homework outside the school with no coat or mittens while the classroom thermometer showed an outdoor reading of – 30 degrees Fahrenheit.

My Grade Five teacher was an imported American, and while I don't mean to imply her imperialistic ways were in any sense characteristic of her countrymen, I can without hesitation connect my own feelings of fervent Canadian cultural nationalism to those endless months so long ago that I spent under her doubtful tutelage.

For one thing, she refused to lead us in "O Canada" in the mornings the way the rest of the teachers did. Instead, she taught us with painstaking meticulousness a new song called "My Country 'Tis of Thee", writing the words out on the blackboard until we had them down by rote. Although, as she pointed out, the tune was the same as "God Save the Queen", I felt sure there was something the matter with this new morning anthem. Not the least of the problem was that it had lines in it about "land of the pilgrims' pride", and I was pretty certain that the pilgrims didn't belong to us.

But when I approached her about this, my teacher's eyes flashed behind their rimless lenses, and she launched into her familiar refrain about how unintelligent Canadian children were, compared to American children. It was a charge

I could not, even then, take seriously, not from a woman – an American woman at that – who professed to believe that the name of the Great State of Iowa was pronounced Eye-*Oh*-Ah.

In the end, I did what any indignant Canadian would do. I complained to higher authorities – in this case, my mother, who was horrified to learn I was singing a song about "sweet land of li-ber-tee", when everyone knew that Canada was not the sort of nation to inspire such a jingoistic lyric.

After my mother in turn complained to the principal – a man, incidentally, whose eyebrows met in the middle and who insisted to his Grade Eights that the synonym for "crazy" was pronounced "lun-*at*-tic" – some changes were made to the Grade Five morning regimen. "God Save the Queen" came in as a hasty replacement for "My Country 'Tis of Thee", although it was a long time before any of us, by now massively confused, could remember to end up with "Go-od save the-eh Queen!" instead of "Le-et free-duh-um ring!"

Meanwhile, my teacher's suspicion that *I* had been the one who'd alerted the Thought Police only exacerbated a relationship already made difficult by the inkspots-on-the-glasses episode. And by the time she discovered that I'd also altered a picture in my social studies textbook so that the overseer of ancient Egyptian pyramid construction looked just like her, the rest of my tenure as a Grade Five student was not worth living, to the point that, eventually, expulsion to the frozen schoolyard seemed a positively balmy fate, compared to the deep-freeze I was experiencing inside the classroom.

It was not, in short, the halcyon experiences of earlier grades, when I was petted and pampered by my teachers, who enjoyed my cheerful eagerness. In fact, my sentence to Grade Five provided my first indication that school could be difficult, and relationships with teachers combative and mutually wary. I began to sense, however dimly, the potential of political leverage available to the trouble-maker, the misfit, the brat, and by the time I got to high school and the restrictive atmosphere of a nun-run life, I had begun to assume that the teacher was the enemy, to be outsmarted and, whenever possible, ignored.

A far cry, altogether, from the good old days – arguably the best old days – of Grade Two, where I was one of thirty or so seven-year-olds who made the inexhaustibly delightful acquaintance of Miss Riley. I frankly loved Miss Riley, and I believe that, to this day, I could pick her out in a crowd, with her red-gold hair and her slightly gummy smile, and her merry laugh which, surely, not even the weight of intervening years could have dulled or diminished.

A significant fact – perhaps *the* significant fact – about Miss Riley was that she had come from England, the first person I had ever met from any place east of Winnipeg. How on earth was it that a pretty (I'm *sure* that she was pretty) and vigorous young woman from Britain should take it into her head to teach Grade Two in a pink-brick primary school stuck, like an eraser on a sheet of foolscap, on the snow-swept Canadian prairies of the 1950s? Miss Riley never said, and it certainly never occurred to us, at the age of seven, that bleak employment conditions in Europe or any other sharp exigency could have had something to do with her decision to emigrate. Anyway, Miss Riley seemed like the kind of person who did things on the prompting of no other impulse than curiosity, enthusiasm, and unbridled high spirits.

Unlike the sour-faced shrew lying in wait for us in Grade Five, Miss Riley *liked* Canada. She even liked Saskatchewan. At least she insisted that she did, as a troupe of us trailed her around the snowdrifted playground at recess, vying and jostling to be the lucky two who got to clutch Miss Riley's Albian hands.

Of course, as she gave us clearly to understand, things were very different in England. In England, she said, little boys wore short pants and knee socks, even in the winter, which struck us as hilarious, although, as Miss Riley pointed out, it wasn't nearly so cold there. Or anywhere.

There were many other things about England that made

it different. What we called a "pullover", girls in England called "a jumper", and what we called a jumper was known there as a pinafore. You didn't play Follow-the-Leader in England; instead, you followed the Bangalory Man. And spring came in March instead of at the end of May, and a robin was a round and rosy-breasted thing, as opposed to the tall, orange-chested bird that we knew, and schoolchildren over there sang songs like "D'ye Ken John Peel" – which Miss Riley duly taught to us, along with the plot of Gilbert and Sullivan's *Iolanthe*, in which she was playing one of the fairies in a local little-theatre production.

What made it possible to learn so much about England and John Peel and Iolanthe was the fact that Miss Riley didn't adhere much to the curriculum. Nevertheless, she made a point of being eager to help us appreciate what our own culture had to offer as well, even if she was a bit vague sometimes as to what that might be.

In order to induce us to brave the sub-zero weather of a Saskatchewan winter recess, Miss Riley awarded a prize each day to the boy and the girl with the rosiest cheeks. She dug out a song called "Land of the Silver Birch" and made us learn it, even though we protested we'd never once seen "the mighty moose wander at will" anywhere in our town. And when the weather finally warmed up at the end of May, Miss Riley insisted that we go on nature hikes around the gumbo-ridden playground so that we could bring back seeds to germinate on pieces of moistened blotting-paper, and neat-looking bugs to inhabit mason jars in the Nature Corner she had instituted at the back of the classroom.

It was the day that the school janitor – a shrivelled but overbearing little German man whom the boys whispered about as a "Not-zee" – threw out our Nature display that Miss Riley lost her temper. She came into our classroom to find him heaving seeds, blotting-paper, bugs and all into a metal wastebasket, while haranguing a frozen grouping of us girls about "brinking zuch mezzy chunk" into the classroom. Her face became as red as her hair, red enough to win any Rosy Cheek Prize going, and she screamed at the janitor in a way that gladdened the hearts of all of us who had been systematically terrorized by him since the first day of Grade One.

But there must have been other irritants than the janitor in Miss Riley's life at our school, despite her perpetually cheerful demeanour. For one thing, our prairie parochialism must have depressed her, in those moments when she found herself missing England most. I remember one day she asked, almost wistfully, whether any of us had been born outside Canada, and one of the boys immediately stuck up his hand to report that his family had come from Estevan.

"Estevan?" You could see Miss Riley brighten with hope, as she contemplated the possibility of some Near Eastern principality, or even a dreary Soviet republic bordering on Lithuania. "Where exactly is Estevan?"

Oh jeez, I thought, what jerks she'll think we are, as I put up *my* hand to let her know that Estevan was close to Weyburn, which was in turn less than two hours' drive away.

Poor Miss Riley. You could tell that she was made both angry and crestfallen by this news, and though she fought to keep these feelings from showing, she virtually snapped at the boy from Estevan, "I said another *country*, not another *town*."

Then there was the time she took it into her head that our Grade Two class should come up with an impromptu entertainment for the edification of the rest of the school, and drilled us in some sort of *cloun-et-mime* dance performed to a scratchy record, after which she assembled all the other grades to watch us perform.

It was a complete disaster. Not only were we under-talented and under-rehearsed; none of the other students could comprehend us as clowns and elves and golliwogs, since we had not a single costume or one prop to our names.

When one of the other teachers professed herself as mystified as the students by our pantomime, I heard Miss Riley wail tearfully, "It's meant to be a work of the *imagination*."

Imagination. A sacred concept to Miss Riley, and no doubt the area in which she benefited pupils like me most. A slave to cigarettes, like most teachers of her generation, Miss

Riley would long to repair to the staff room for a restorative puff, and quickly learned that the accepted trick was to leave a moderately entertaining student in charge. That student, in our Grade Two class, often turned out to be me.

I could read well enough to march importantly up to the front of the room and prattle speedily through whole chapters of *Black Beauty*, while somewhere off-camera, Miss Riley smoked, and while the rest of the class alternately sighed and cheered, depending upon whether the news for Beauty and his friends Ginger and Merrylegs was bad or good.

My task became more difficult once *Black Beauty* had been laughed and cried to a conclusion; Miss Riley handed me another horsy story about the highwayman Dick Turpin and his courageous mare, Black Bess, before heading off to the staff room, her deck of Sweet Caporal cork-tips peeking from her pocket.

Dick Turpin and Black Bess made a wonderful story; it was only when we came galloping to the end that I got into trouble. It seemed that Dick Turpin had been forced to ride his steed mercilessly to elude a trap set by his enemies, and as we neared the conclusion, Black Bess was winded and close to collapse, while my classmates were on the edge of their chairs.

As I read aloud in an excited treble, my eye went racing ahead to the last paragraph, and I saw some fateful words that indicated the heart of the noble horse was about to burst from her exertions. I couldn't stand it. I clapped the book shut, and started to cry.

"What's the matter?" the rest of the class demanded.

"Black Bess!" I bawled. "She dies!" And immediately the entire class, even the boys, burst into sobs. Poor Miss Riley came hurrying back from the staff room, stale cigarette smoke clinging to her jumper or pullover, to discover her Grade Two class collectively awash with tears.

The wages of imagination were not always so traumatic. Sometimes, when Miss Riley needed a cigarette or had piles of marking to do, she would set me up at the front of the classroom with a piece of chalk in my hand to tell the class an illustrated story. As I recall it, I would have no idea, when I set out, where the story was going to come from, or where it might go. I would merely begin talking, and temporizing by drawing pictures on the blackboard as fast as I could to bring to life the characters I was talking about. Eventually, I guess, I managed to weave a story, cobbled together from fairy tales and TV and whatever else came to mind, that would come to a convenient conclusion whenever Miss Riley's assignments were done.

I never had, before or since, a teacher so encouraging of my enthusiasm for inventing stories on the spot. Nor a group of classmates so appreciative of the efforts I made to beguile them. No wonder the news, at the end of the year, that Miss Riley was leaving our school came as a cruel devastation.

Why she'd chosen – or had it chosen *for* her – to leave, we never found out. Was it as a result of having screamed at the janitor? Or was it because she'd mistakenly addressed the visiting Archbishop as "Mr. Grace" the day he came to our school? Had the failed clown-and-elf pageant inspired anger along with derision in the other teachers? Or was it, perhaps, that Miss Riley's enthusiasm for piercing prairie winters was less unbridled than she'd pretended?

Our class, of course, bought Miss Riley a gift on the last day of school. But my best friend and I, motivated by our superior love, decided to pool our savings to purchase for Miss Riley a present of our own, something worthy of her charms. There was a garish yellow plaster spaniel on sale at Lakeview Hardware, and we bought it, and took it to Miss Riley on the last afternoon, long after everyone else had left the school.

It was scaldingly hot, the way days could suddenly be on the prairies at the end of June. The desks, I remember, reeked of the Lysol we had all been compelled to clean them out with earlier in the day. I found myself dizzy, both from the emotion of the moment, and from the smell.

Of course Miss Riley loved the plaster spaniel (what she called a "figguh" and what we called an "orn-u-ment"). It was exactly what she'd always wanted, she said. I felt thick-tongued and sick-hearted, trying and failing to articulate to her what she'd meant to us, how I'd miss her, how devastating it was going to be to go into Grade Three, where nobody would ever trust me to step up to the front of the class and concoct a story, illustrated in chalk. So, after some desultory chit-chat, my friend and I left Miss Riley – to dispose of the "figguh", I now assume. I went home, flushed and wretched, to bed, where I remained, physically sick with my grief, for several days of the summer vacation.

The weather continued dizzyingly hot. In a vacant lot across the street from our house, construction was in progress, with huge machines droning an accompaniment to my delirium. I dreamed Miss Riley hadn't left after all, but each time I awoke, confused, soaked with sweat and with Caterpillar tractors grinding in my ears, she was still gone. Each time that happened, I would burrow back down into the sheets, to dream about her once more, overwhelmed by the first separation of my entire life.

The separations, of course, have come again and again since, although none, perhaps, with the impact of that first piercing loss. Predictably, I have often wished I might run into Miss Riley again, or even hear news of her whereabouts. Oh, I know she is not Miss Riley any more, probably not even in name. Nor crowned with a mane of curly red-gold hair, nor young and sprightly and defiant of the stodgy ways of a prosaic little pink-brick school stuck on the grey-green lapel of the prairie like some prosaic orn-u-mental pin.

But I still dream that now, if I saw her, I might make her understand how the oxygen of imagination she breathed into our circumscribed lives gave me lasting hope. How much I valued the opportunity she gave me to beguile others by making things up.

And how, in the end, I admired her for daring to be quintessentially, if sometimes erroneously, herself – in an environment that decreed, with dull regularity, that one should always be anything but.

Mona's Manners for Married Men

I'm sure you too have a friend like Mona. Not only does Mona specialize in futile relationships with married men, she also specializes in *complaining* about her futile relationships with married men.

At first, I and her other friends took it for granted that married men must be what Mona wanted, in spite of her complaints. After all, we'd sneaked enough checkout-line peeks at *Cosmo* to know that whatever happens to women they generally bring on themselves, through a combination of bad attitude, bad nutrition, and bad choice of accessories.

But then meetings with Mona became so unremittingly depressing that it was impossible for us to imagine that she was only pretending not to have a good time. Her life was a continual chronicle of married men who neglected to phone her or to leave their wives, who promised the moon and failed to deliver so much as a moonstone, who gave her excuses instead of their hearts, and who turned up unannounced and disappeared without a trace.

So you can understand why it was with gloomy trepidation that I agreed last week to meet Mona for dinner, and why it was with intense surprise that I spotted her in the restaurant looking sleek, bright-eyed, and hugely satisfied with herself.

What on earth had happened? Had she finally fallen for someone unattached? Collectively told her bevy of married men to go to hell? Succeeded in persuading one of them to drop his wife at last?

"None of the above," Mona smiled smugly, pulling from her purse a pile of manuscript pages and spreading them on the table in front of me. "All I did was sit down and write a book."

Indeed she had. *Manners for Married Men* was typed on the title page, and the whole stack of paper must have been at least two inches thick.

"The publisher is crazy about it," Mona murmured modestly. "And they paid me a fifty-thousand-dollar advance."

As I leafed through the typewritten pages, I could understand the publisher's enthusiasm. Mona's book covered all of the basest bases of married-man management, every single one.

"Do's and Don'ts" one chapter was headed, and the list was practically endless. "When staying over at the home of your out-of-town girlfriend, *don't* criticize any decor or furnishings you aren't prepared to pay to see changed. She does not need to hear you marvel how *anyone* can get along without an ecologizer, when she herself is getting along without a full-time relationship, and she should *not* be encouraged to run out and buy things to make her place more comfortable for you. Such behaviour smacks too strongly of the nesting instinct, which, given the situation between you, is strictly for the birds.

"*Do* keep your mouth shut about your wife, mindful that no matter how you talk about her, it will backfire. Not only does your girlfriend not want to hear what a marvellous woman you are cheating on, she would be equally unhappy to be told that the only reason you're here is that any alternative, however paltry, is a vast improvement on your pitiful home life."

Mona's book also contained Travel Tips ("When taking your girlfriend on a trip, remember that jotting your romantic dinner down as a 'Miscellaneous Business Expense' will only depress her") and A Checklist of the Ten Stupidest Questions ("Do you mind if I call my wife collect from your place?").

Then there was a Compendium of Useful Phrases for the First-Time Philanderer. "Of course I meant to tell you right away that I was married, but I was so bowled over by you, it completely slipped my mind." As well as, "No matter what, I promise I'll never hurt you." And finally, Mona's own all-time favourite, "I'll see if I can slip away while she's trimming the tree to give you a call."

But I would have to say that probably the most useful section of *Manners for Married Men* was the "Glossary of Terms" Mona had laid out to assist married men in choosing their words with maximum tact and minimum legal liability.

"*Soon* – An adverb as convenient as it is indeterminate, as in, 'I'll be moving out of home soon,' and 'I got here as soon as I could.'

"*Perfect* – A good word to invoke when you want to keep things from moving along too quickly. 'But darling, how could our relationship be more perfect than it is right now?'

"*Here* – A vague little monosyllable with a thousand and one marvellously evasive uses. Examples: 'Just being here with you is enough for me.' 'I don't know what I'm asking, except that you just be here for me.' Or 'Come on, I'm *here*, aren't I?'"

I closed the manuscript and shoved it back across the table to Mona as I chuckled with appreciation. "It's wonderful," I said. "I hope you make a million bucks."

Mona dimpled demurely. "Well, doing the research was no picnic, but writing it was an absolute snap. And you want to know the best part?"

"Sure. What?"

"The best part is, once *Manners for Married Men* hits the streets all my problems are going to be solved. After the book is out, there won't be a married man out there who'll come near me with a ten-foot pole."

Lorelei, Lucy, Lassie, and Lulu

For those women honest enough to admit that they remember the 1950s, it's become a habit to blame that mean-spirited decade for all of the failings of ego and identity we continue to suffer to this day. It's a tempting thesis. Just look at the view the American mass media of the fifties offered us little girls of our proper sphere and probable future. There was Marilyn Monroe as Lorelei Lee insisting that men grow cold as girls grow old (I can't imagine where she got an idea like *that*). And Lucille Ball pulling self-deprecating *moues* every time her husband Ricky smacked his brow in exasperation and shrilled "Ai-yi-yi!" at another one of her blunders.

Speaking of television, though, it may be that the most pervasive influence of them all on kids of the day was *Lassie* – not so much the dog as Jeff's mother. (What *was* her name, anyway – Ellen? Mostly we thought of her as Mom, pronounced the American way, of course, as in Somerset Mom.) Jeff's maugham wore high heels with her aprons. She baked endless pies and shook her head indulgently at Gramps as he toiled over his checkerboard, while *she* toiled over everything else on the farm that needed doing.

Some things, however, were beyond even Jeff's mom's twinkle-eyed capabilities. Things like bad bears sighted on the back forty (forty *what*?) and Gramps trapped under a tractor on the same back forty while the camera cut back and forth between him and the bears. On those occasions, Clay Horton, the State Trooper (whatever *that* was), had to be summoned, by Jeff's mom ringing down to Gertie at the switchboard.

Not that Clay Horton ever turned out to be a blind bit of use in those situations. Oh sure, he was earnest and solicitous and obviously in love with Jeff's mom – who, as a farm widow, had just as obviously interred her heart in the same back-forty pasture as that in which Jeff's father had doubtless been laid. So Clay Horton never got to first base with Jeff's mom. And of course he seldom solved the central dilemma of the show either, because that particular task was always left up to Lassie.

Lassie? I hear you interject. Now, wait a minute, Lassie always saved the day, and Lassie was a *girl*. Surely that constituted a positive female role model for girls growing up in the fifties?

No. Sorry. Lassie may have been nominally female, but it was generally known to kids in North America that the dog who played Lassie was actually a succession of dogs, and that each and every one of those dogs was a *male*. Only boy dogs, it was understood, had the intellectual capacity to master all those stunts.

All of the above being the case, how was it the fifties managed to preside over the production of today's adult women, who are basically a pretty good crop? Where was the positive influence countervailing the negative impact of the Loreleis, the Lucys, and the Lassies? I'll tell you where: In *Little Lulu* comic books.

I've been looking over yellowed back issues of *Little Lulu* lately. You'll be relieved to know that she stands up brilliantly to the rigorous scrutiny of the eighties, her political resolve as tightly coiled as the black springs of her Scarlett O'Hara ringlets.

Consider the cover of the September 1951 *Little Lulu* comic, where Tubby, Eddy, and the rest of the Clubhouse Boys dressed in cowboy gear threaten Lulu with their cap guns. Unbeknownst to them, the invincible Lulu is reaching into her doll carriage to produce a bug-sprayer. Again and again Lulu meets mindless might with resourcefulness, compassion, and wit. When she is drafted to play football with the Clubhouse Boys – who don't want her, but need her to fill out the roster – Lulu is the one who carries the day by stealing the pants of the opposition, the overbearing Westside Gang, thereby causing them to run off the field in disarray.

Even in her fantasies, she is unflappable. As she imagines herself as the Poor Little Girl being imprisoned in a rock by the evil Witch Hazel, she also imagines herself reacting calmly with the mild remark, "This is the funniest thing."

Which is not to suggest that everything comes easily to the sharp-nosed girl in the red dress. The boys continually refuse to let her or any of her girlfriends into their clubhouse. Little Alvin, the youngest boy in the neighbourhood, is already man enough to evince boredom at Lulu's epic tales of Bad Witch Hazel and The Poor Little Girl. And Lulu fails to get a date for the party at Miss Gladys's dance school because Gloria, her blonde and politically incorrect rival, has wheedled all of the boys into inviting *her*.

Nevertheless, Lulu prevails by coping, and manages to cope without losing either her dogged idealism or her ironic sense of humour. And what a relief it is to rediscover Lulu more than thirty years later, and still find in her someone modern women can continue to emulate in everything except dress style. It may be true that Little Lulu never succeeded in persuading the boys to let her into the clubhouse. But perhaps she accomplished something more important in the end. She may, for all we know, have helped a whole generation of girls to begin to learn that the world that really counts is the one *outside* the clubhouse.

The
Realest
Woman
of
Them
All

Time was, serious arguments used to range around what constituted a Real Man. Did he have to be taciturn and full of *machismo* like Hemingway, or was there still room in the manly pantheon for the kind of guy who wasn't ashamed to admit he liked Debussy and knew how to cry?

Well, the jury never did come back in on that one, because a far more politically sensitive question intervened: Namely, what constitutes a Real *Woman*? Is she out wheeling and dealing in the boardroom all day, serene in the knowledge that all is quiet on the domestic front in the competent hands of the day-care staff and the maid service? Or is she home where she belongs, whupping up a batch of muffins with which to lobby the anti-abortion vote of her local male politician, who – chances are – hasn't had any home cooking since his wife deserted the family for that real-estate course?

If only the indignant feminists and the righteous traditionalists had come to *me* before the controversy got out of hand. I could have told them exactly what a Real Woman is and, by way of illustration, proffered the life story of Myrna Hemmingstitch, the realest of all the real women.

Although born in the mid-western United States, Myrna Hemmingstitch came to Canada as a young woman, to serve a journalistic apprenticeship on the *Toronto Daily Star Home Companion*. It was here, according to literary scholars, that she not only honed her characteristically terse prose style, but also came upon a recipe for Foolproof Pot-roast.

In her free time, Myrna Hemmingstitch roamed the sanely laid-out streets of Toronto – although, of course, only during daylight hours, and never without her hat and gloves. Her diary chronicles both the positive and the negative aspects of Toronto in the 1920s.

"Often I go to Murray's, and at Murray's it is the tea that seduces the heart. It is said of the tea at Murray's that it is like a coy mistress, who alternately kisses and slaps you. Of the tea at Murray's it is said by the old ones that it takes the enamel from your teeth and leaves it on the roof of your mouth. I think, another time, I would add some milk."

And yet for all its allure, Toronto was not enough for Hemmingstitch, who, at the soonest available opportunity, was on a ship for Paris – hoping to make it in time for the unveiling of the Spring Collection, and unaware that Toronto was on a land-locked lake. But after a disappointing arrival in Kingston, she was soon on her way once more, to France and posterity.

In Paris she located the expatriate community, who immediately took her up. They put her down again, however, just as quickly when Hemmingstitch started criticizing the cookery section in Sylvia Beach's bookstore, Shakespeare and Company. The Fitzgeralds, for their part, soon tired of Myrna's mania for sewing on buttons whether they were loose or not, and even James Joyce had trouble keeping his temper when they visited Versailles, and Myrna's only comment was, "Gee, I'd hate to have to wash all those windows, wouldn't you?"

Again, it is her diary that serves as the most reliable index of her lonely alienation. "Soon, with the literary community, it all falls into a rut. You drop over to see Gertrude Stein, and that is fine, except that Alice B. Toklas is putting what looks like oregano into the brownies, and you try to talk her out of it. And she gets angry, and you both drink too much and quarrel, and soon one of you ends up with a black eye. When you try to tell her a bag of frozen peas will take down the swelling faster than anything, she laughs and does not believe a word you say.

"Then, when you pass this hint to Ford Madox Ford, who has dropped over to complain about the silliness of his name, he tells you to shut up with your handy hints, and not to bother telling him how to get the soup stains off his shirt. Then you *do* tell him, and you quarrel because you have both had too much to drink, and one of you ends up with a second black eye, and there is another bag of peas in the freezer that is cold and green and does the job."

But without a doubt it was Spain, not France, that really formed Myrna Hemmingstitch into the Real Woman we revere to this day. Not only did she write some of her best work there – including stories like "A Clean, Well-Lighted Place in Five Easy Steps" and "A Way You'll Never Beat Carpets", and her first novel, *The Bun Also Rises* – but her diary also reveals the extent to which the visceral aspects of Spain and the suffering of the Spanish people helped to shape her prose and her character.

"We walk into Pamplona and it is hot and dusty," she declares in her diary. "And I wonder how I will manage to press my cotton sundress. Then the bulls begin running through the streets, and I ask my compadre, 'Who will clean up after them?' Joyce does not answer, but this is no surprise. Joyce has not spoken to me since Versailles."

It was in Spain that Myrna learned everything there was to learn about life and death and war and peace, as well as the secret of packing and repacking a suitcase. It was in Spain also that she learned to love everything about bull-fighting except, as she wrote, "the smell, the noise, the dirt, the blood, the crowds, and the animals". She wondered how the proud matador managed to launder his Suit of Lights without electrocuting himself. "I want to find out. I might ask Zelda Fitzgerald, but Zelda does not know important things like that. Zelda is not, I think, a Real Woman at all. The only things that Zelda knows are how to dance on the roof of a taxicab without snagging her hose, and where on the Côte d'Azur it is possible to get a gin fizz served to you on the beach.

"Scott, on the whole, knows a lot more about things than Zelda does. But after a few drinks he forgets everything he knows, including the correct temperature at which to wash woollens. I have told Scott that if I see him in one more pair of shrunken plus-fours, my gin fizz will be in his face."

Despite her impatience with the feckless Fitzgeralds, Myrna Hemmingstitch derived much of value from her stay in Europe. Not only did she complete another novel, about a tragic relationship between an English army nurse and a young American furniture refinisher in war-torn Italy (*A Farewell to Armoires*), but she began to make preliminary notes for what undoubtedly stands as her greatest literary work, *For Whom the Jell Moulds*, a comprehensive look at cooking for large international brigades during a civil war.

Much – far too much – has been made of Hemmingstitch's irascible temper and regrettable tendency to turn on those who had helped her most. Certainly her memoir of expatriate life in Paris, *A Movable Feast for Twenty or More*, contains some scathing references to people like James Joyce and Gertrude Stein, who had been her benefactors. But what her critics fail to note is the hundred and one little kindnesses the well-built authoress performed for those she thought of as her friends. Again the copious diaries are the best source of information on this topic.

"Ezra Pound dropped over today, still raving about Mussolini and fascism and all that other stuff that doesn't matter. Tried to set him straight on what life is really about, without much success. We argued half the night, drinking all the while, of course, swapping punches. My punch was made from fruit juices, grenadine, and sliced lemons, with the touch of club soda that hits the spot. Again and again I tell myself to write down the exact proportions before I forget.

"In the end, little headway made with Pound. He still drinks and raves that he can wear that striped sports jacket with houndstooth slacks. 'Look, Ez,' I said. 'At least admit that the brown shoes have got to go.' He won't, though. Too stubborn – or maybe, now, too crazy."

On the romantic front, literary pundits have commented on Myrna Hemmingstitch's seeming inability to sustain a marital relationship. But, far from reflecting negatively on her claim to Real Womanhood, Myrna's multiple marriages actually enhanced her image as a truly feminine being, tirelessly dedicated to the principle that a woman's true role and proudest vocation is to make a home for her man, regardless of how many homes and men that might entail.

The fact was, both Hemmingstitch's breath-taking womanliness and her prodigious domestic drive together conspired to make it difficult for any man to keep up with her. Affectionately known by the Spanish as *muchas parabolas* ("she of the extraordinary chest"), Myrna not only was possessed of a figure that could (and more than once did) stop the running bulls cold in the streets of Pamplona, but exhibited a real mania for housework that proved, in the end, too much for her succession of spouses. One by one, they dropped away from her, either tired of trying to think up new compliments for her seven-layer torte, or else weary of endless disagreements over whether ironing jockey shorts was absolutely necessary or not.

Still, Myrna Hemmingstitch had her fame to console her, and it did. As the realest of the Real Women said of herself in her last diary entry, shortly before succumbing to a self-inflicted wound from a frosting-gun, "Next to cleanliness and godliness, there is a prose style so clean that, beside it, traffic signs read like Thackeray. Yes, I've had it all."

Submissiveness Training

I guess it's no secret that I don't know how to flirt. In fact, I have no secrets at all, which may be one of the problems. To be truly flirtatious, I feel, requires among other things an air of mystery. My life is an open book. A book of trigonometry, which may be another of the problems.

In any event, there are those women who are born knowing how to flirt, and those women who are not. Up until recently, I believed there was absolutely nothing that those in the second category could do to elevate themselves to the first.

After all, the differences obviously run far deeper than the mere capability of blinking one's eyelashes rapidly and to effect at men. Women who flirt are also the sort of women who remember to keep a fragrant sachet in their sweater drawer. When travelling, they always bring along a tube of travel soap, with which to rinse out a few things. Unlike the rest of us, they only ever *have* a few things that need rinsing. And these few things, needless to say, are packed neatly along with some carefully co-ordinated separates into a set of matching luggage.

But please don't get the idea that Women Who Flirt are a bunch of swooning Victorian belles. These gals play a mean game of tennis or golf, and never ever get headaches from the fetching coloured sweat-bands that they wear while playing. They invariably remember to laugh when they muff a shot, their noses don't sunburn, and by dint of toothy good-sport smiles, they never have to wait more than a few minutes to get on a court or to the tee.

I wish I could tell you that Women Who Flirt lose it completely when they head home to cope with domestic life. But they don't. Somehow or other, a Woman Who Flirts can dash around her house for eight minutes with a Dustbuster and a can of Florient, and have the place ready in case the Royal Family drops in unexpectedly for smart drinks. When the entourage does arrive, she flirts expertly with the Prince of Wales and the Duke of Edinburgh, and yet manages not to alienate either of the wives, who end up begging her for her guacamole recipe.

But perhaps it's at work that the W.W.F. assert their true superiority over the rest of us. I'm talking, of course, about women who remember to bring along a toothbrush to clean their teeth after lunch, while the rest of us resort to gargling away the effects of a garlic pizza with the fluid that runs the Xerox.

Learn to spot the W.W.F. in your office by noting who doesn't need to keep a pair of comfortable shoes in a bottom drawer. Women Who Flirt can walk endless miles of office corridor in heels so high that oxygen may be required, and still manage to smile. Their pantyhose never snag on file-cabinet corners; age cannot wither the flowers at their work stations, nor typewriter keys chip the lustre of their nail polish.

It would be easy to hate these women, were they not so

damned nice. Their Christmas lists run in excess of four hundred gifts, including presents for the shrew in Accounts Receivable, for your shut-in aunt that the w.w.f. has never met, and for the entire population of a Third World village. Somehow all of these presents – which invariably fit – get purchased on one lunch-hour in October and mailed off the same day.

As I said right at the beginning, I used to believe that Women Who Flirt were born, not made. That was before I happened to spot a tiny advertisement nestling in a remote corner of one of the back pages of a neighbourhood newspaper.

"Too blunt?" the ad suggested quizzically. "Devoid of Charm? Utterly Lacking in Feminine Wiles? Fret no more, because you too can earn big compliments in your spare time by Learning How to Flirt! It's easy, it's fun, and it stands a girl in far better stead than a course in actuarial calculation. A new semester of courses begins this week at the Institute of Submissiveness Training. Drop by any time for a free evaluation of your Coquetry Quotient."

Well, what can I say? I was desperate enough to try anything. And what I learned by dropping into the Institute promises to change my life so radically that I feel compelled to communicate the details of the experience to you. I must warn you, however, that should you decide to follow my lead and head down to the Institute of Submissiveness Training, don't expect to be bowled over by appearances. From the outside, the institute is not an imposing place. In the foyer, however, hang commanding portraits of Scarlett O'Hara, the Gabor sisters, Mata Hari, and other inspirational figures in the history of flirtation. There's also a glass case in the hall, displaying a collection of sticks donated by graduates who found that they needed them after completing the course to beat off hordes of inflamed men. Otherwise, there's not much physical evidence of the principles to which the school is dedicated, or outward manifestations of the type of work that goes on there.

Trust me, however. The work itself is formidable, and indeed nothing about the Institute of Submissiveness Training is easy. I could tell that the minute I came face to face with the Institute's director, Bambi McCoy, Professor of Flirtation Emeritus.

Bambi (as she insisted I call her, with a winning dimpled smile) is everything you'd expect of an accomplished Woman Who Flirts, and much much more. Not only was her caring femininity evident in the picture of Mother Teresa she wore in a locket around her neck, but Bambi also had enough black mascara on her eyelashes to resurface the Macdonald-Cartier Freeway, and wore a fragrance so alluring than even another woman would feel compelled to buy her lunch.

But Bambi wasn't interested in my offer of lunch. What she wanted from me were answers to the Submissiveness Training Questionnaire, devised to pinpoint the particular areas of flirtation in greatest need of repair.

Question One: You are at a sporting event, and notice an attractive man who seems to be alone sitting a row or two ahead of you. Do you: (a) throw your hotdog at the back of his neck to get his attention? (b) smile at him on your way to the washroom, and when he fails to smile back, dismiss him as an obvious homophile? or (c) stop beside him on your way back from the concession bar, offer him a cup of beer, and say, "I always buy a drink for the best-looking man in the stands"?

Question Two: You are standing in line at the bank machine. The handsome guy standing behind you remarks, "This automated world we live in is so impersonal, isn't it?" Would you: (a) answer, "Yes, thank God, otherwise I'd be forced to deal with schmucks like you"? (b) immediately notify the police that someone is trying to pry your Secret Access number out of you by coercion? or (c) smile sweetly and say, "What an original thought. I've never looked at it that way before"?

Question Three: You telephone a friend, and find yourself chatting with her single brother visiting from out of town who is, according to her reports, "one of the last of the good ones, and he's willing to relocate." When he invites you over to wait with him for your friend to return, do you: (a) bring four of your best-looking girlfriends along with you for protection? (b) go over alone, but ignore him while you chat to the fantail guppies? or (c) chat and laugh with him animatedly till your friend comes home, whereupon you and her brother announce your engagement?

Well, what can I say? To none of the above questions did I answer (c), and Bambi immediately assigned me to the Special Learning class that she personally presides over to help those with more pronounced flirting disorders.

The course is called Elementary Flirtation, and as Bambi told us on the first day, the initial and also the hardest step on the road to coquetry is to admit aloud: "Yes, I am a failure as a flirt."

It wasn't, as you can imagine, easy for me to stand up in front of a roomful of strangers (even strangers as charmlessly unintimidating as myself) and own up to a thing like that. It's no snap to hear yourself recount aloud your social failures, and believe me, my voice faltered as I told the group that the last time I winked at a man, he immediately reached for the Murine, thinking I had a cinder in my contact.

Indeed, it took every ounce of courage I possess to reveal that my idea of hinting for a date is to snarl, "Call me up, if you want to see your mother alive," while I tend to march up to every new male possibility with all the coy indirection of a streetcar, wearing a pressed-on smile and a frank stare, and proffering a firm handshake that gives the initial impression I have arrived to show him some real estate.

Still, Bambi had heard many agonized confessions as pathetic as mine, and probably a lot worse. "Now, class," she soothed the group (consisting only of me, a female bouncer from a bikers' bar named Killer, and a woman who'd worked as Margaret Hamilton's stand-in on *The Wizard of Oz*), "The first thing we're going to do is measure you for dimples like mine, which will be surgically implanted after the class. Of course, false eyelashes are regulation school wear, as are pearl initial pins and a Laura Ashley tote bag. Then, once you're properly attired, we will videotape you in a number of standard flirting situations, in order to show you the mistakes you're making."

Well, it was a pretty punishing experience, I can tell you,

the first time I saw my flirtation failures brutally replayed, accompanied by Bambi's running play-by-play. "Now, class, note the way she's entering the party – not smiling and open, and eager to see and be seen. Not at all. Why, she's just prowling around the edges of the room, isn't she, like a coyote skulking the prairie in search of wounded grouse.

"And – uh-oh, here she is, attempting to make conversation over the dip. Hands up, anyone who can spot the error here. Yes, that's right, Killer. She's so nervous, she's dipping a coaster instead of a chip.

"But she's hanging in, isn't she, trying to socialize. Now, what's going on here? Right, trying to make desperate small talk with a strange man by asking him the square root of twelve!"

Bambi has assured me that she is humiliating me only to help me, and she points for inspiration to the example of the female bouncer. Even Killer has now learned there are more enticing ways of starting a conversation than by slapping a man across the back and demanding, "So, Shorty, how's it hanging?"

Anyway, I'm determined to stick it out, and by the time I make it out of Elementary Flirtation, through Intermediate Innuendo, and perhaps even into the half-course the institute offers in Advanced Archness, who knows? The day may not be so far away when I learn how to drop my handkerchief in such a manner that the man who picks it up and returns it to me has other things on his mind than a citizen's arrest for littering.

The Chain of Command

With no intention of getting Freudian about it, I must report that I've always had an uneasy relationship with keys.

It all stems from my childhood, when I was practically the only kid on the block who owned a key to the house and used it regularly. When I could find it, that is. Even back then I could always be counted on to lose a key as soon as look at it, with the result that I was constantly to be found at the back door of neighbours' houses, knocking anxiously and shifting from foot to foot in the unmistakable two-step of a child desperate to use the bathroom.

My mother used to sling the key around my neck on a string, which was fine until the string broke in the middle of a softball game, and I'd end up in the thickening twilight,

anxiously sifting through the dust of the ball diamond, paus-
ing only to shift from foot to foot in the unmistakable two-
step of a child desperate to use the bathroom.

Later, when I was older and supposedly more in control
of my life and my bladder, I was issued a blue leather zip-
up keycase in which to keep my house key, as well as the
key to the lock on my bike. Unfortunately, one Saturday
afternoon at the movies, I ate the entire keycase (except for
the metal spine and the zipper) as a nervous response to the
tenser moments in *Pyscho*, and walked home with tell-tale
blue-leather dye stains around my mouth, hurrying in the
unmistakable two-step of a child desperate to use the bathroom.

Needless to say, the keys had gone missing on the sticky
popcorn-studded floor of the movie house, never to be seen
again.

As an adult, I can't claim that my luck with keys has
improved much. I have been known to get myself into such
a temper while ramping around the house in coat and boots,
searching fruitlessly for the keys, that I actually seize the
cat by her furry lapels, shake her, and demand, "Come on,
where are they? You must have seen me put them down.
Now, spill it!"

It was precisely this sort of near-psychotic behaviour that
led to my acquisition of a Talking Key Chain, which has led
in turn to the terrible chain of events I'm about to recount.
The principle of the Talking Key Chain is in fact pretty
simple. You attach your keys to the thing, and when the keys
go lost, as keys invariably must, you – as Lauren Bacall had
it in *To Have and Have Not* – just whistle. Thanks to two tiny
magical batteries, the chain then emits a shrill answering
warble that enables you to pinpoint its location.

The little charm worked like a charm, for about a minute
and a half. Sure, it would answer every time I whistled. But
almost immediately it began driving me dotty by also
answering every other high-frequency sound that went off
in the house: the cat's meow, the whistle on the tea-kettle,
even certain notes blown on the stereo by Wynton Marsalis.

Next thing you know, the key chain started piping up
whether it was asked to or not. I'd be hunting around the

living-room for the newspaper or a mislaid bottle of nail polish, and the chain would begin chirruping from the mantel: "Getting warmer, getting warmer – whoops, no, cold now."

Soon, as you can imagine, I was utterly dependent on the Talking Key Chain to organize every aspect of my disorganized life. Not only did I find myself begging it to divulge the whereabouts of my stamps, gloves, and dictionary, I was asking it whether I should take my umbrella, take an Aspirin, take the car.

The chain was only too happy to trill its high-pitched opinion, but, knowing it had me where it wanted me, it also began making exorbitant demands. First, it asked for (and got) a talking bathroom scale for "company", although how something that recites "Your weight is fifty-two point three kilograms" in a nasal monotone could be construed as company even for a key chain is anybody's guess.

When the chain petitioned for a talking clock and one of those telephones that warbles like a hummingbird on bad acid, I drew the line. Or tried to. Because when I put my foot down, the chain retaliated by refusing to tell me where I'd left my bankcard, and whether my blue sweater was dressy enough for a dinner party.

In the end, of course, one of us had to go, and since I am bigger, it was the key chain who finally left.

Not without some regret on my part, I have to say. Life is quieter now, and many things in the house go lost once more. I've reverted back to my childhood habit of wearing my key around my neck on a string, still with very limited success. And I sense that the bathroom scale misses the key chain too; although it won't divulge anything more than "Your weight is fifty-two point three kilograms," I notice that it does so in a more subdued tone.

As for the key chain . . . Well, things seem to be going very well indeed. The last I heard, my Talking Key Chain had a syndicated talk show all its own. Upcoming programs, according to the TV schedule in the paper, will include thrilling chatter with a cellular phone, a drop-in visit by a family of ruby-throated warblers, as well as an in-depth interview with the car from *Knight Rider*.

FUN ON ICE

Let's face it. Some ice sports are more absorbing than others to watch on TV. Take curling – knowing that if you do, you will be in a small and exclusive category of people who would also probably enjoy televised presentations of manuscript illumination. For most people, curling just isn't a sport with breath-taking visual appeal.

In the first place, it's hard to feel excited about a game that's played in tams and patterned cardigan sweaters. I'm not sure why this is, but as long as we're on the subject, the same kind of wardrobe complaint can be levelled at golf, another sport that, to put it crudely, sucks the big one on the small screen. In fact, when you come to think about it, the kind of folks who curl in the winter are very probably the self-same individuals who choose to golf in the summer, and in both cases you get the persistent feeling that someone from the Kiwanis came by to distribute the clothes.

Even the terminology of curling doesn't lend itself to high television suspense. Playing an "end" has a defeated sort of ring to it, almost as if the outcome were either predetermined or inconsequential in the face of graver considerations. "Lead rock", despite its musical connotations, doesn't necessarily sound like an event you want to be around for either, while somebody called the "skip", who hops around excitedly brandishing a broom, quite honestly belongs more legitimately in the chimney-sweep number in *Mary Poppins* than in TV sports drama, where leading the team on to sudden-death victory is the desired dénouement.

Having said these withering things about televised curling – and you are, by the way, free to disagree with me – let me quickly go on to announce that I've found another sport, performed on thin ice, that lends itself much more readily to dramatic television spectatorhood. Like curling, this thin-ice sport is open to both men and women, although there is no team competition as such, except in the Pairs Events. Otherwise, the emphasis is on Men's and Women's Singles. My kind of game.

If you haven't guessed already what this visually dazzling and nerve-shatteringly demanding sport is, just listen for a minute to the audio tape I made of two colour commentators discussing a recent Men's Singles event at an international championship broadcast live on TV:

"Well, of course, I know that both for fans at home and the eager crowd thronging the bleachers here at the stadium in Dubrovnik, this next contender is the one we've been waiting to see perform his Compulsory Figures in the Men's Singles event. Kevin, wouldn't you say that this is the contender the fans have been waiting for?"

"Actually, Doug, as a former champion myself – "

"Yes, Kevin, of course, I forgot to mention that. Former Canadian Men's Singles Champion Kevin Horner is with me, folks, here in the broadcast booth to provide some psychological texture for us on what these young contestants are going through. Now, remind me, Kevin, what year was it you took the Men's Singles crown?"

"It was 1975, Doug, although it feels like only yesterday, I must say. Anyway, what I wanted to point out is, it's not really the compulsory figures the crowd waits to see, it's the free-style program that will follow, a program that the contestant has designed for himself. Although, even in the compulsories – "

"Yes indeed, Kevin, you're absolutely right. Now, our young hopeful of the moment, a highly favoured contender, I might add, has made his appearance and indicates he's ready to begin. This is Canada's own Wayne Dorgreb, of Kindersley, Saskatchewan. Kevin, what do we know about him?"

"Well first, Doug, what I was starting to say is that in the compulsory figures, we really see the backbone of any competitor's style. Each of the young men in contention today has been asked to perform the following program in sequence: a bluff, a feint, and a double dare, followed in rapid succession by excuses, first on the telephone, then face to face, and then, to finish, the breath-taking triple take, where he must act surprised over something he knew very well all the time. It's a formidable program, Doug, and I'll be interested to see how young Dorgreb handles – "

"Kevin, he's already finished his bluff, in the form of a bland assurance to his boss that the Marsden Project will be on his desk by Tuesday – "

"Yes, a bluff that he chose to perform over the phone, by the way, Doug, which is absolutely permissible. But – "

"But now he's well into the feint, a fairly conventional grab for the cheque in a restaurant, Kevin, making it a bit too obvious, I'd say, that he intends to let the client pick it up."

"Yes, Doug, I'm afraid Wayne Dorgreb is going to lose valuable points with the judges for the transparency of that feint, but oh – look how he's handling the double dare! You know, I can imagine just what's going through his mind as –"

"He's onto the closing series of figures now, Kevin. We've had the telephone excuse, pretending to his fiancée he has a cold, beautifully executed, and now he's telling the boss a big dog ate the Marsden Project. . . . Gosh, Kevin, I don't know if the judges, particularly the Russians, are going to go for that, do you?"

"It's a very, very difficult manoeuvre, Doug. Nobody outside this kind of competition really understands *how* extremely difficult, but I think I have to agree that – "

"And now, the final, the triple take. . . . Yes, we see him stop and look surprised when the boss tells him he's through. Now he's starting for the door – stops, shaking his head, stunned. He turns back now, as if to protest, starts to walk away and – oh, beautiful move, and just listen to the crowd! Turns *back*, Kevin, for one more incredulous look! What a triple take! Have you ever seen a triple take executed more beautifully than that?"

"Doug, now I'm beginning to see why Wayne Dorgreb is being touted as the logical successor to the style I made famous, and I'm doubly curious to see how he does in his free-style program later. The numbers are coming up now – "

"Five-eight, five-eight, five-seven, five eight, five-six – "

"The Russian judge, of course – "

"Five-eight and a five-nine from the Scandinavians . . . very promising beginning for Canada's own Wayne Dorgreb. But now, coming up, we have Leonard Stork from Esher, Great Britain, who is – "

"Leonard Stork is, in my opinion, Doug, the man to beat this afternoon. He's completed his compulsory program already, and consistently pulled numbers of five-point-eight or better, even from those Russian judges, and what he's lined up for himself in his free-style program is so utterly challenging that I'm hard put to believe he – "

"As you said, Kevin, Leonard Stork is on deck right now, looking anxious in a blue silk shirt and darker-toned blue fitted pants, as he views to cement the title for Great Britain, which, if he does, will be the first time in a long while that – "

"Doug, excuse me, but I absolutely feel that before Stork commences his program, our audience must be made aware of exactly what it is about his intended sequence that makes it so utterly special. He is – "

"Kevin, you've been in this spot in the past. Waiting to present yourself in front of an international crowd with some daring and quite possibly controversial manoeuvres. So why don't you give the viewers at home some idea of what Leonard Stork plans to do and why it's so goldarned unique?"

"What a good idea, Doug. Why don't I do that? Let me say that everything, absolutely everything Stork is presenting this afternoon is off-beat and chancy. For instance, he intends to start, right off the bat, with a bold presentation of his résumé. This is, of course, very seldom done, particularly by British competitors, notoriously conservative in their presentation. Not even the Americans in contention here began their programs with their c.v.'s, if you'll remember. The Americans both started off by presenting their cards, a fairly conventional opening move, and only worked up to an offer to *mail* the résumé, and that was well into the program."

"Right you are, Kevin, and it may be worth noting here that the Canadians have been more tentative still. Not one of them even included an offer to mail a résumé at any point in the free-style program."

"Well, that may be more of a comment on the postal service than anything else, Doug. Because, by the same token, you'll notice that each of the Canadians' programs has featured at least one dazzling move involving the sending of important work-related documents by courier."

"Yes, I recall that was an element in *your* program too, Kevin, although we're going back a few years. Amazing how little has changed since then."

"Well, of course, I only gave up international competition six years ago, Doug. It's hardly an eon. But what I was trying to tell you about Stork from England is how *many* risky departures there are in what he plans to show us. For instance, he will follow a broken engagement *immediately* with an impulse marriage – very seldom successfully attempted – and he then proposes to attempt to execute a *quadruple*-cross on his new bride, something, quite frankly, that no one has been able to pull off, either competitively or even in a practice session, in front of the bathroom mirror."

"Hold it, Kevin. You'd better explain the complexity of the quadruple-cross, before we – oh, too late. Stork is beginning his program. The silken strains of 'My Way' are pouring out, the music he's chosen to open his program, and he has no trouble at all with that résumé presentation, Kevin, as unorthodox an opening move as it is."

"Yes, he's got the brashness to pull it off, and I don't expect him to be in any trouble, Doug, until he hits that quadruple-cross, which must be preying on his mind, even at this early point in his plans, as he executes a nice but fairly routine triple take – "

"Some applause from the crowd, of course, who acknowledge a good triple take, as Stork pretends to fail to recognize an old school pal in the street, then acknowledges him, then realizes it's someone he owes money to, and protests that he must run to catch his bus. Beautiful sense of balance on that triple take, Kevin, he didn't falter once."

"He's too smooth to falter this early, Doug. Notice him now, closing a deal at a bar with faultless grace, and at the same time, almost in the same movement, planning to make an approach on a pretty girl he's noticed out of the corner of his eye. I like the musical shift at this point, too, from 'My Way' to the Pachelbel 'Canon', just to ensure an illusion of sensitivity and depth."

"Will he really try that quadruple-cross though, when he has everything to lose? That's what this crowd wants to know."

"I think he'll try it, but if he doesn't make it, the crowd may be disappointed, although I don't think it's going to hurt him that much with the judges. Nobody really expects that combination to work, Doug, it's just fiercely complicated. First, he has to bring off that broken-engagement–sudden-marriage sequence. Then he has to follow up on it almost *immediately* by cheating on his wife with the boss's secretary, which is the double-cross; then, wheedling important company documents from the secretary to discredit the boss at the stockholders' meeting; and *then* somehow or other manage the quadruple-cross by starting an affair with the secretary's best friend without the secretary finding out and blowing the document bit. I don't know, Doug, I – "

"Well, Kevin, here it is, he's into that combination. The double-cross . . . working fine, the little woman none the wiser. Now on to that board meeting for the triple. . . . So far so good, and here comes the secretary's best friend into the – Oh. Oh gosh. Well, what a shame."

"What did I tell you, Doug, going for the quadruple was just too much for Stork. There's the best friend on the phone to the secretary, and with that, Stork has taken a bad spill, a very bad spill indeed. He's up on his feet very quickly, though, and moving on now, totally unruffled, into a beautifully executed reconciliation with his wife and a job interview at a new company using falsified references, which is a nice touch. He's finished well, but what thoughts must be going through his head!"

"Yes indeed, Kevin, he's bound to be disappointed, despite a strong response from the crowd. Leonard Stork of England. We're waiting to see how he's been scored, and later on in the competition we'll look forward to seeing him perform in the Pairs Event with British compatriot Audrey Wadsworth Sim, but for now – "

"Audrey will be fascinating to watch in her own right tomorrow, Doug, in the Women's Singles. Not as flashy as the men's events of course, but what the ladies lack in dash, they more than make up for in neurotic self-deprecation. I'll never forget the free-style program Audrey Wadsworth Sim presented in Stuttgart, two years ago, when she opened with that breath-taking spiral right onto the bed, as a reaction to Mr. Right phoning her up with an invitation to dinner."

"That's right, Kevin, who can forget it. Although my own favourite moment in her program that year had to be that Triple Lux. Do you recall that Triple Lux at all?"

"Oh, of course. When she was so nervous about her upcoming wedding she absent-mindedly took three showers right in a row. The crowd was ecstatic. As always, though, what sticks in *my* mind are the less showy but more difficult sequences.

"For instance, there was the boring date, which she got out of early by yawning and claiming extreme fatigue. Then, when her date let her off at her front door, she walked into the house and straight out the back door, without missing a beat, to hail a cab and head down to a jazz club for a late drink. A very difficult moment ensued, you'll remember, Doug, when she ran right into the guy who'd driven her home a half-hour before. But she recovered marvellously by telling him she'd gotten her second wind and had come down to the club on the chance he might be there. Then, at the end of the program, she dumped him again. What a combination of moves! The Stuttgart crowd was on its feet for a good two minutes."

"Yes, Kevin, lots of fun to be had tomorrow, in the Women's Singles. For now, though, we're still awaiting that score from the Men's Singles and – "

"And I for one have had about all the drama I can take for today, Doug."

"You can say that again, Kevin. For Kevin Horner, this is Doug Melling saying, don't go away, folks. After a brief commercial word, we'll be right back with more breath-taking live competition from the international world of Skating on Thin Ice!"

Grounds for Discourse

I don't want you to get the idea that I've received some kind of financial consideration from the Coffee Growers Association to extol the merits of their product. As a writer – and let me state this categorically – I cannot be bought. (Unfortunately, according to my agent, I cannot be *sold* with any degree of facility either, and he's rapidly becoming concerned that I probably cannot even be given away.)

No, the only thing that prompted me to discuss the subject of coffee with you was an interesting little statistic that came across my desk the other day. Since so often it's interesting little insects that come across my desk, I was sufficiently motivated by the comparative novelty of a statistic to pay close attention. The statistic was this: While the most popular non-alcoholic beverage in the United States is cola, in Canada it is coffee.

Gee, but that small unspectacular fact cheered me. I can't honestly explain why, except that I have long believed in coffee as one of the cornerstones upon which this society rests. What the other cornerstones might be, I can't, just offhand, venture to say. I think Canada Savings Bonds could be one. Or a free toque with every fill-up. Or the inviolable principle that the nine Kurdistanis with expired passports will always be in the Canada Customs and Immigration line just ahead of you when you are arriving back home on a delayed flight at midnight from the worst business meeting in Cleveland you've ever had.

Anyway, as statistics show, coffee is a beverage of enormous centrality to the concept of Canadian consciousness. Indeed, it's arguable that coffee is the one thing that keeps us conscious as a people at all.

Personally, I think the key to coffee's success in this country lies in its sublimely non-threatening character. Think about it. Back in high school or college, when someone new and attractive sidled up to ask you if you wanted to "have a coffee", what did it really mean? Something promising, perhaps. But nothing irrevocable, nothing that either or both parties couldn't deny later if necessary. A coffee, in fact, could mean *exactly what you wanted it to mean.* Just that much and no more. What an exquisitely Canadian drink – one that manages to be both casual and meaningful at one and the same moment.

In the adult world, coffee continues to perform the same soothing social function. Ask an interesting stranger out "for a drink" and you may be asking for trouble. There's something a little suggestive about a drink, isn't there? Something slightly leering, indicative of knowing winks and insinuating manoeuvres under the table.

"Lunch" is no solution either. Lunch, in fact, is far, far worse. Only former roommates and members of the Mafia ever manage to pull off lunch with any degree of success.

The rest of us squirm in tortured agonies wondering what kind of permanent effect creamy tarragon dressing might have on gabardine, and why the other person did not think highly enough of us to ask us out for dinner.

Not only does an invitation to a coffee work wonders in tentative social situations, but you can tell an awful lot about somebody in an awful hurry merely by noting the kinds of choices they make when confronted by a cup of black coffee. Let us count the ways:

One cream, no sugar. Yes, this looks like a promising, well-balanced type. While the use of cream betokens the agreeable impulse to smooth coffee's (and life's?) rough edges, there is still ample indication of someone who is willing to let coffee be coffee, without undue tampering.

Double cream, no sugar. Uh-oh. Could be getting into the realm of the control freak here. I mean, if *this* is how the person feels about coffee, why didn't they order a mocha milkshake instead?

Double cream, double sugar. Oh, please. Talk about double trouble. All the preceding comments about double cream apply, with an added caveat: Watch out. You could be dealing with someone who can't face reality *at all.*

Black, no sugar, Whoops, steady on. Too far in the other direction. No desire here to put a stamp of individuality on their coffee or themselves. Probably the type who cooks up Kraft Dinner exactly according to the specifications without inspired additions, and owns a dog named Rover.

Black, with sugar. Weird, definitely weird. Oh sure, they'll do some astonishing things to Kraft Drinner, and the pet named Rover is probably an ocelot, but are you sure you can cope with someone who demands such mutually contradictory things of their coffee?

One cream, one sugar. The aptly named "Regular". No flashes of originality here, but at least likely to be less morose than the Black, No Sugar type. Known to put bits of chopped olive into the Kraft Dinner in a mad moment, and seriously considered calling the dog Major before settling on Rover.

Well, I don't claim it's foolproof as a method of character assessment, but at least it's a beginning. Besides, so what if your cup of coffee with this person turns out to be a long cold drink of water? Remember, coffee commits you to nothing. Just don't let some American ask you out for a Coke.

The
Schleppy Woman's Guide
to
Money Management

I realize that I'm not the first person who's thought of offering women their own guide to sound financial management. If wooing women to part with their money has become big business in the affluent eighties, counselling them on exactly *how* to part with it is even bigger. You'll see handy manuals on every airport bookshelf and every drugstore display rack, proclaiming woman-tailored advice on making investments, playing the stock market, making out a will, and starting up your own business. And these books are all well and good, in their way.

The only thing wrong with them, really, is that all of them are intended to appeal to only one kind of woman. I think you know the kind I mean. The kind of woman who thinks of herself as "savvy" and organizes her life accordingly.

The savvy woman is the one who wears big shiny button earrings, patterned stockings (without runs), and a blouse (clean) with a self-tie. She carries an ox-blood leather investment binder tucked under her left arm, and a Burberry raincoat slung over her right, and hanging from her shoulder of choice is a large, expensive handbag on which the clasp closes with a prosperous-sounding "snck".

Well, you know me. I wouldn't for one minute dream of putting the knock on savvy women. They are, unquestionably, what the struggle for liberation was all about, and also what assures the continued relevance of Holt Renfrew in an otherwise changing world. It just so happens that I don't know any savvy women personally.

The women of *my* acquaintance are all more or less like me. By which I mean they're *schleps*.

Now, *these* are the women crying out for help. These are the women in dire need of some advice, any advice, on what to do with their money. Because the fact that they are *schleps* in no way implies that they are penniless. Far from it. *Schleps* often have more discretionary income than they know what to do with. It's just that phrases like "discretionary income" cause their throats to constrict and their pulses to race. This is because *schleps*, although seldom born moneyed, or rarely having achieved money through canny hustling, very frequently have had money thrust upon them. Usually by the simple and embarrassing expedient of having earned it.

And now they are walking around town in their runny pantyhose, with their wrinkled Fairweather raincoats slung over their arms, a respectable-sized wad of the folding green folded up in their battered canvas Garfield shoulder-bags, and a permanent air of bewilderment. All because these chicks simply don't know what comes next. However, they will soon. Just as soon as *The Schleppy Woman's Guide to Money Management* comes on the market.

The first thing the book will do is to warn the schleppy woman about the kind of people money is going to bring into her life. Which is why the very first chapter is headed "Choosing an Accountant". It opens as follows:

"The first thing to remember is that accountants, like dentists and undertakers, are people no one looks forward to visiting, and accountants know it. This makes them defensive about the dullness of their profession, which in turn causes them to treat every conversation as if it were a Vegas lounge act. ("Now, take your money – and I plan to!") Accountants will also always encourage you to have 'fun' with your money.

"There is, of course, no such thing as having fun with money, unless you are the type who likes to fold dollar bills so that the Queen's face winds up looking like a rude part of the human anatomy. Be warned, therefore, that an accountant's idea of fun will be very different from yours.

"In fact, his notion of a high old time is advising the tax-deductible acquisition of some piece of work-related equipment as unnecessary as it is mystifying, or counselling you to drop in on a trust company to inquire about self-administering RRSPs. Fun? You bet."

Of course, once the schleppy woman has an accountant and once that accountant has brought people like trust company managers into her life, she will then encounter a whole array of baffling new terminology that requires explication. This is where *The Schleppy Woman's Guide* is once again worth its weight in investment tax credits (whatever *they* are).

Chapter Two is a glossary of some of the more abstruse financial phrases:

"*ROB*. The section of the *Globe and Mail* they put the 'Cathy' cartoon in, for the same reason your accountant tells bad jokes – to give you the erroneous impression that money people have a sense of humour.

"*Roll-over*. What the mining stock you bought on a tip from your accountant's cousin does just before it dies.

"*MURBs*. Little blue gnome-like characters that feature prominently in Saturday-morning cartoons, and have spun off successfully into key chains, car-mirror ornaments, and lunch-pail decals.

"*Fixed interest*. When interest rates fall too fast (before 'bottoming out', in technical monetary parlance), they can often fracture in the process, and must then be repaired by the Governor of the Bank of Canada. He uses a special alloy of secret ingredients, and once interest has been fixed with this mixture, it is referred to as *compound interest."*

Ultimately, though, merely learning the words will not suffice, unless you're also humming the tune. What the schleppy woman must grasp, above all things, is the principle that principal is inevitably going to change her life, will she or no. That is the proposition upon which the closing chapter of the book is predicated, with its handy Before-and-After checklist of pre- and post-money phraseology.

BEFORE MONEY	AFTER MONEY
postal money order	certified cheque
sandwich at your desk	working lunch
old Hills Brothers coffee tin	safety-deposit box
rust out	depreciate
fall fashions	new bond issue
handout	interest-free loan
teabags	T-bills
savings-account book	investment portfolio
therapist	stockbroker
lottery ticket	real-estate speculation

In the end, of course, it's all far more trouble than it's actually worth. Nothing in this world comes to us without consequences, as the schleppy woman will discover when she begins to notice that the car her money brought into her life requires repairs far more often than her old bicycle. Thanks to her new-found affluence, there is a cleaning-woman brooding over soap operas in the living-room like Napoleon on Elba, when she is supposed to be dusting the unsightly but tax-deductible "work station" the schleppy woman's accountant urged her to set up in the den. Worst of all, the schleppy woman has endured so many working lunches that the phrase "stock option" automatically makes her think of arugula.

At this point, the schleppy woman becomes a candidate for the sequel to *The Schleppy Woman's Guide to Money Management.* It will be called *The Schleppy Woman's Guide to Money Mismanagement,* and will outline ways to reclaim a former life of impecunious merriment by disposing of all cash and investments by various brutal, unequivocal, and senseless methods.

Amazing Urban Bicycle Stories

Whenever cyclists get together after a hard day's ride, to take off their pant clips and put their feet up in front of a fire, you can count on the conversation to revolve around just one topic: the distinct and remarkable personalities of their individual bicycles.

"Me, I'm inclined to tie one on from time to time," Wilf confides guilelessly (and unnecessarily) as he pours himself yet another glass of Selectionné. "'Course, if I tried to drive my car home in that condition, I'd be a dead duck for sure. But on my bike? Hey, no problem. I just give 'er her head and she takes me straight home."

Brenda replies that her own two-wheeler – a spirited little

Motobécane – not only has the same homing instincts, but exhibits qualities of extraordinary loyalty as well. "I've tried lending my bike to other people, right? Forget it. It absolutely won't go into the higher gears for anyone but me."

Well, of course, the one or two sceptics in the group start to chortle at this, but Cecil silences them with a story both eerie and touching, even to those of us who've heard it many times before.

It seems that Cecil was pedalling down a deserted country road one fall when the brakes on his Bottechia began to lock inexplicably. "It didn't matter what I did, eh? Every few feet the damn thing would come to a screeching halt and refuse to move."

Finally Cecil climbed off and continued along the road, walking the bike beside him. "Even at that, though, it didn't seem to want to go down that road at all. And guess what? A few yards later I found out why. The bridge was washed out. If I'd been gunning along top-speed, we'd have gone in the drink for sure."

But perhaps the most affecting tale is Barry's, about the beloved bicycle he had stolen from his backyard more than two years ago. With tears in his voice, he tells us how the bicycle thieves repainted it, then sold it to an unscrupulous bicycle courier outfit. After hard use there in all weathers, the poor machine fell into the hands of a grocer's helper, who attached a delivery basket to the front and rode it mercilessly.

At last, at a neighbourhood garage sale, the abused bicycle became the property of a child who loved it and treated it with care. It was at that point, by sheerest coincidence, that Barry and his purloined pal were reunited.

"See, I went to the Fall Fair in the park, and when I passed by this one parked bike, it fell over – all by itself. And this piece of paint chips off, and right away I recognize it. It's my old bike! I was never so happy in my life. Only, the little kid who owns it, he's so upset when I tell him it was stolen, I haven't got the heart to take it away from him."

"What a guy," Wilf murmured reverentially, pouring himself another glass of Selectionné.

But I really must assure you that there is more to these bicycle-appreciation evenings than inspirational anecdotes and pathetic self-indulgence. We also discuss, with vociferous enthusiasm, exactly *how* bicycles accomplish their anthropomorphic marvels. On these occasions, it's my heartfelt contention that bicycles learn from other bicycles.

"It all became clear to me," I inform the others, "when I started working at a regular day-job, which meant locking up the bike in the same communal rack day after day. Once my bike began associating with the same group of other bicycles on a daily basis, it was utterly incredible how many new things that CCM learned."

By way of example, I tell them about the weeks my bicycle spent fastened beside a baby-blue ten-speed Peugeot, and how it subsequently emerged from the experience fluent in French.

"A bilingual bicycle," Wilf remarks. "I'll drink to that."

Then there was the stately Raleigh from which my bicycle learned to recite the entire succession of the British monarchs, as well as acquiring a truly delicious recipe for Battenberg cake.

"Oh, come on," says Barry uneasily. "That's a bit far-fetched."

Not at all. Lest they think I'm boasting, I hurry to assure them that I haven't always been entirely thrilled with the kind of stuff my bike's picked up in the racks. "Like the mountain bike with knobbly tires and eighteen gears that taught my bike the most appalling mountain-man manners, not to mention how to yodel.

"And then there was that swaggering know-it-all Schwinn from the States that started making fun of the way my bike says 'out and about', and 'chesterfield' instead of 'sofa'. Eventually they wound up in handlebar-to-handlebar combat over the free-trade issue."

Well, at that moment I perceive that I've lost even the most credulous bicycle-lovers with that one, but I swear it's all true. And I know there will be cynics out there who will doubt the veracity of *all* amazing bicycle stories, even those as tame as Wilf's and Brenda's.

But for those of us who know bikes, and who ride them with love and respect, there will always be room in our hearts to entertain any evidence that attests to the special intelligence of our chosen mounts. These are not, I assure you, mere dumb vehicles. While the car has the horsepower, the bicycle wins it every time, handlebars down, in good old-fashioned horse *sense*.

The   Lance

of

the   Free

Doktor, I had it again.

JA? YOU MEAN FISH FOR LUNCH?

No, no. The dream. The recurrent one, the one that drives me crazy.

UND SINCE WHEN DO YOU DECIDE WHAT IS CRAZY AROUND HERE?

Anyway, you know the dream I mean. Where I'm a free-lancer again, stuck home working all day, with fifteen hundred empty Humpty-Dumpty Krinkle Kut Potato Chip bags for company and a mile-high stack of projects all promised for next Wednesday.

I am in the process of noting that not one of them has been developed beyond the stage of a three-and-a-half-by-five-inch file card with "Help!" written on it when the phone rings.

I spring to it, hopeful of a wrong number with whom I can pass a pleasant hour or two chatting, or perhaps one of those nice market-research people who have so often brightened my solitary afternoons with solicitous inquiries about my preference in breakfast foods.

But no. On the other end of the phone is my agent, anxious about another of my projects, promised for last Thursday, which still languishes on my desk in the form of another of those three-and-a-half-by-five-inch file cards, this one marked "Big Trouble".

"So," he begins, trying to sound casual, "how's it coming?"

"Terrific. Almost virtually finished, practically. Nothing left but those little touches of detail – like the plot, characters, setting, and dialogue."

"Uh-oh. It's that bad?"

"It's worse. Look, do what an agent is supposed to do."

"You mean lie? I did that already, last week."

"I prefer to think of it as covering for me," I say.

"I did that last week, too. Now I'm going on vacation."

"Now? When I need you?"

"I'm an agent. That's precisely when we go."

"How did I get so over-extended? It's those cards you had printed up for me. 'Have Pen, Will Grovel.' Now every producer and editor in town thinks I aim to please."

"Just give me a date to tell them. When do you think you can have a first draft?"

"That depends. When do ice-skates go on sale in hell?"

Eventually I get my agent off the phone, but the dream goes on. I'm back at my desk, trying to come up with a few witty lines with which to greet the mailman (the only flesh-and-blood person I'm going to see all day) and debating whether it's worth shaving my legs for the typewriter. That's around the point I wake up in a cold sweat, Doktor, screaming, "I tell you, I finished the work, but a big dog ate it!"

HMM, JA. I REMEMBER NOW. UND WHERE IS IT COMING FROM, THIS DREAM?

Come on, we've been over this terrain a million times. My unresolved feelings about abandoning the free-lancing life in favour of a full-time job.

UNRESOLVED? I DON'T GET IT, SCHATZIE. IT SOUNDS RESOLVED TO ME. YOU HATED WORKING AT HOME.

No! There were terrific aspects to it, too. Like the utter freedom of going into an empty bank at 2:34 in the afternoon for a leisurely chat with the tellers. I didn't even *own* a bankcard, and the only lineups in my life were outside the Odeon on a Saturday night. There were no crowded laundromats back then, or hot subway cars packed with people in coats that smell like wet Weimaraners.

HMM, JA. UND SO . . . IF IT WAS SO TERRIFIC, THIS FREEDOM, WHY DID YOU GIVE IT ALL UP IN THE FIRST PLACE?

Doktor, where have you been? I explained all that, with the dream. Why I had to go out and find a job, or go nuts.

UND SINCE WHEN DO YOU DECIDE WHAT IS NUTS AROUND HERE?

Look, it's a *conflict*. That's a word that must have come up in one of your classes at the Institute or wherever you took your training.

RADIO COLLEGE OF CANADA. I GOT ABNORMAL PSYCHOLOGY AND RADAR TRANSMITTER MAINTENANCE ALL IN THE SAME SEMESTER. IT WAS A PRETTY GOOD DEAL. UND SO TELL ME, LIEBCHEN –

Holy jeez, is that the time? Sorry, Doktor, I don't have time to try to explain my conflict any further. I've got to get to the office.

GOTT IM HIMMEL. AT THIS HOUR? IT'S ONLY SEVEN-THIRTY.

I know. Except that before I go in to work, I have to fit in a fitness class, hoof it down to the shoemaker, stock up on some stocks at my broker, cut in to the hairdresser, then step on it to make an appointment at the auto-repair shop. All of this before nine o'clock. I won't even tell you what my schedule is like *after* work. Now can you understand my conflict?

JA, WELL, MAYBE. COULD YOU TAKE THE DREAM AGAIN, SLOWLY FROM THE TOP?

I'll save us both some time, Doktor. I've composed a little poem that pretty much covers the whole thing:

"O say, does that tear-spangled battle yet rage,
'Tween the lance of the free and the slave to the wage?"

I LIKE IT, MEIN SCHATZ, I LIKE IT. SAY, YOU EVER THOUGHT OF BEING A WRITER?

Say goodnight, Doktor.

Stephanie Leacock: Unmasked, Considered, and Appreciated

Like any writer in this country who aspires to the label "humorist", I have read the works of the master, Stephen Leacock, with real avidity, hoping to glean somehow – perhaps by a sort of literary osmosis – the secret of twinkle-eyed comic prose.

But in the midst of a recent perusal of Leacock's work (including his social criticism as well as his comic pieces) I was stricken all of a sudden with a feeling of uneasiness. What could the feeling mean? I did not know. Nevertheless, I continued in my reading, hopeful that the underlying cause of my sense of cosmic wrongness would eventually make its way up to lie on top. And eventually it did.

Suddenly, right smack in the middle of a joyous re-appreciation of Leacock's political-economy text *Responsible Government*, I was struck by a blinding revelation: *The work had been written by a woman.*

That was it. That was the one discordant element that continued to niggle in an unquiet corner of the mind. That was the precise source of my extreme unease. That was the kicker; that was what was wrong with this picture. Stephen Leacock hadn't written Stephen Leacock's work. A woman had.

Well and good. But *what* woman? That burning question drove me through exhausting months (well, minutes, anyway) of research. And the startling fruits of that unflagging quest I humbly submit for your consideration: Stephen Leacock had a *twin sister* who ghost-wrote every single piece of his work.

Leacock's sister was named Stephanie, and she was born – coincidentally – on exactly the same day as her more famous twin, in 1869. Even more uncannily, like her brother, Stephanie also emigrated from England at an early age, to settle in Sutton, Ontario.

Ironically, it was here, in a New World supposedly awash with fresh opportunity, that the real inequities between Stephanie and her sibling began to show. While Stephen, the male child, was sent, first, to Upper Canada College and then to the University of Toronto, Stephanie was forced to teach herself economics and political theory at home, aided only by a Bible, an old Farmer's Almanac, a geometry text, and a battered copy of *More Jokes for the John.*

It is a lasting tribute to her persistence and ingenuity that from these unlikely sources flowed her masterful humour, her terse, economical style, and her astounding social acumen – qualities, unfortunately, destined to twinkle faintly for most of her life from under a bushel of bristling male chauvinism.

EARLY ACCOMPLISHMENTS

One day in the early 1900s, fresh out of embroidery twist and looking for something to do, Stephanie sat herself down in the family garret at the escritoire she'd fashioned for herself out of a peach crate, to do a little of what she called "doodling". By the time she rose from her labours a neck-crunching twenty-two hours later, Stephanie had penned most of what became the basis for *Elements of Political Science*, the first of her many books. Formidable doodling indeed.

Yet her attempts to get the book published under her own name met with failure. Editors in Toronto and England were openly derisive in their replies to Stephanie's polite inquiries as to their interest in bringing out a new Canadian text of political science.

"Come, come, my good woman," ran a typically patronizing response from a senior editor at Frippery and Son, Number Eight, The Old School Tie Road, London. "Can you seriously expect this esteemed firm to cast even a cursory eye over a manuscript on such a weighty theme submitted by a female? A volume of cookery, by all means. Pretty fairy-tales for the nursery, certainly. We would even look with favour upon a knitting manual forwarded to us by one of your tender sex. But the rigours of political science, my dear, are not a fit topic of consideration for those of your gender. Please do not trouble yourself or us with your submissions on this subject again."

Stephanie kept this sniffy dismissal, just as she kept all the others, carefully folded and pressed between the covers of her dog-eared old copy of Euclid. And while, externally, she showed no evidence of her discouragement, internally how she must have chafed at the humiliation!

It is not surprising, therefore, that after a succession of such rebuffs, Stephanie decided on another course of action in order to help her manuscript to see the light of day.

While Stephanie had slaved in the garret over *Elements of Political Science*, her twin brother Stephen, after lounging his way through his courses at the University of Toronto, had become a lecturer in economic theory. But he still devoted more of his time to tending his moustache than to tending his class, and spent hours cracking billiard balls together in the Masters' lounge when he should have been cracking books. Talk about Lazy Leacock was rife and hostile. In his Department there were increasingly bitter suggestions that if he didn't get some tract or monograph in his field published fairly soon, Stephen would be turning in his academic gown for overalls, and his mortarboard for a trowelful of mortar.

Hence, when his sister Stephanie approached him with the tentative suggestion that he permit her to append *his* name to the title page of a scholarly manuscript, Stephen was more than happy to comply.

The rest, of course, is Canadian academic history. With a male name on the cover, *Elements of Political Science* was snapped up for publication in 1906, and the following year, *Responsible Government*, also penned by Stephanie, met the same felicitous fate. Virtually overnight, Stephen Leacock, stagnant student and lacklustre lecturer, was transformed into a respected author of comprehensive and scholarly textbooks.

GROWING DISCONTENT

On the surface, Stephanie reacted positively and philosophically to her brother's sudden glory. On the inside, however, she was festering with bitterness, anger, and cynicism over the closed-shop realities of the male-dominated power structure of the day. That bitterness began to ferment in her 1907 essay "Greater Canada", also published under Stephen's name, of course.

To the casual reader, "Greater Canada" appears to be nothing more than a nationalistic rallying-cry for greater Canadian independence within the British Empire. However, a more thorough perusal of the piece reveals the subtext of feministic rhetoric cleverly laced throughout the work by a woman disillusioned with her subordinate lot, yet determined to exploit the advantages of her underground situation by dipping the pen of her conservative brother into the ink of radicalism, much as a politically astute ventriloquist might preach subversion through his dummy.

It was, in fact, my initial encounter with "Greater Canada"

that helped crystallize my conviction that the Leacock canon was female-authored, and it was through exhaustive examination of the essay's taut text that my portrait of Stephanie's character and personality began to form. The work is peppered with derisive references to "ignorant colonial *boys*" (italics mine) and with stinging indictments of the male political establishment that point unmistakably to the gender of the writer.

Consider this scathing sentence that appears in "Greater Canada": "Harsh is the cackle of the little turkey cocks in Ottawa fighting the while as they feather their mean nests of stick and mud high on their river bluff." Not only is Stephanie's angry feminism evident, but she also displays a perspicacious anticipation of the controversies in our own day surrounding political figures who renovate their official residences at the public's expense.

Those who *still* question a woman's authorship of this essay are directed to the unequivocally female phrasing of such word choices as "a widow's mite" and "the vexed skein of our colonial and imperial relations". Such incontrovertible evidence should allay any further doubts on this score.

NEW DIRECTIONS

Despite her brother's usefulness as an unwitting cat's-paw with which to tweak the male establishment, Stephanie nevertheless found it impossible to restrain her resentment at the enormous public acclaim he enjoyed for scholarly works that she herself had written. Consequently, she made a decision to try once more to be published under her own name. Between 1908 and 1910, we find Stephanie attempting to exploit the gimmick-crazed market of the pre-First World War period by producing how-to books. Indeed, there are reasonable grounds to believe that Stephanie Leacock may have invented the how-to form as we know it.

She was by now spending her summers in Orillia, Ontario – as was her brother Stephen, who had, as usual, followed in her wake. Stephanie quickly noted what an exercise-conscious town it was, as well as a town obsessed with superstition. As a result, she sought to capitalize on a fertile market by producing a book of astrologically based calisthenics for the local inhabitants, which she entitled *Sun Sign Stretches for a Little Town*.

Flushed with a sense of accomplishment at having produced a book at such high speed, Stephanie barely paused for breath before plunging into her next project, which showed that her long-stifled interest in economics had managed, slowly, to revive itself. The book was an advice manual for wealthy newly-weds on how to utilize investment techniques first developed by the French settlers of the Maritime regions of Canada. The somewhat unwieldy title she chose was *Acadian Debentures for the Bridal Rich*.

Alas, calamity once again befell Stephanie when she submitted these works for publication with the by-line "Stephanie Leacock". Not only did potential publishers worry that the similarity of her name to that of the (ironically) famous Stephen Leacock would create confusion, but they also short-sightedly refused to anticipate the strong market potential in the how-to genre Stephanie was pioneering. Indeed, several of the responding publishers stated with great vigour that a book of instruction on *any* subject would never sell.

Reluctantly, Stephanie turned once again to Stephen to "front" her manuscript for her. But a surprise awaited her. Stephen, now puffed up with pride at the success of the books whose true authorship he'd conveniently forgotten, refused to associate his name with either *Sun Sign Stretches* or *Acadian Debentures*. Instead, he insisted that Stephanie rewrite both as books of humorous essays, and alter their titles sufficiently to permit their re-submission to the publishers under his name.

Sick at heart but with her back to the wall, Stephanie had no choice but to comply. She made the adjustments Stephen had asked for, thus producing two books of humour so famous that their titles hardly require reiteration here. Significantly, Stephanie detested both *Sunshine Sketches* and *Arcadian Adventures* from the outset, and the greater the fame that accrued to her brother on their account, the more she repudiated both volumes as shallow, toothless, and excessively twee. Strangers who visited the Leacock home in Orillia to pay tribute to the renowned humorist were often struck by his twin sister's sniping, derisive attitude toward the great man's witty essays, an attitude they automatically ascribed to petty-minded jealousy. If only they had guessed at the true and terrible story!

Frustrated in her literary ambitions, forced into the background while her undeserving twin basked in the limelight of public acclaim, and embittered by the seemingly endless injustice of it all, Stephanie fell into the habit of seeking revenge on Stephen by giving interviews to inquisitive members of the press that would reflect unfavourably upon Canada's best-loved humorist.

"Stephen was nice enough as a boy," she told the *Peterborough Inquisitor* in 1915, "but he's grown up into a complete idiot without one original or uncalculating thought. Why, any fool can see he stole that bushy-moustache idea from Mark Twain, and more than once I've caught him practising his merry twinkle in the mirror."

A SEPARATE PEACE, OF SORTS

However, for a woman of Stephanie Leacock's integrity, enterprise, and real generosity of spirit, it was of course unthinkable to content herself with sniping from the sidelines. Therefore, it's not surprising – in spite of the unbroken string of rebuffs dealt to her in the past by the literary establishment – that we should find her, in the 1920s, once more embarked upon the hazardous task of taking the world of letters by storm.

In fact, some things *had* changed since the pre-war era in which Stephanie had first tried to make her mark with economics texts and how-to books. There was cause for her to feel encouraged by the success being enjoyed in the United States by such *soi-disant* "female scribblers" as Anita Loos, and by the more prestigious comic offerings of the increasingly celebrated Dorothy Parker.

Although by now approaching the age of sixty, Stephanie Leacock determined to take this tide in the affairs of women at the flood, and to cash in on the new, more lenient social attitudes toward her sex by resuming her attempts to publish her work under her name instead of her brother's.

Stephanie had, however, learned much from her years of frustrated disappointment, and was not about to run the foolhardy risk of trying the waters with something so weighty as an economics text or a book of political theory. Rather, she elected, with the remarkable shrewdness that characterized many of her career decisions, to stick to a less-threatening vein – namely humour. While still keeping up with the task of churning out economics lectures and comic pieces under Stephen's by-line, she also managed somehow to write – and see published! – her hilarious send-up of Canada's male-dominated drapery industry, *Gentlemen Prefer Blinds.*

While the book received very little notice in Canada or anywhere else – perhaps because of the too-narrow focus of its subject matter – Stephanie had at least succeeded in the cause to which she had dedicated her life: namely, to appear in print under her own name.

But what was Stephen's reaction to his sister's emergence as a star in her own right? We do not know for certain, although an oblique reference in one of Stephanie's letters contains a hint of sibling rivalry. "As for Stevie-baby," Stephanie scrawled in haste to her editor in Toronto, "well, he was fit to be tied when the ten author's copies of my book showed up in the house. 'Call this a *book?*' he demanded, weighing a copy of *Gentlemen Prefer Blinds* in a critical hand. 'Why, consarn it all, Steffie, there's no more heft to it than a drink coaster. I can crank out more prose than that in a single afternoon, and *still* prepare an economics tutorial for my students at McGill.'

"What Stevie forgets, of course, is the reason he's been able to write and teach simultaneously all these years is that *I've* been doing all his ghost-writing. Lord knows who in Montreal he's conned into doing his ghost-*teaching!*"

But whether or not her brother approved, Stephanie was bound and determined to embark upon the literary life, with all the glamorous trappings so long denied to her as Stephen's shadow. Noticing that American humorists seemed to have good times in groups, she attempted to organize a series of Square Table luncheons, at the gracious old Mohawk Hotel in Orillia. To that end she set out to ring the table with a party of witty Canadian notables.

This, it turned out, was more easily said than done. After much consideration, much revision of the guest list, many invitations, some follow-up phone calls, and a quick consultation of a menu-card-sized volume called *Who's Who in Canadian Humour*, Stephanie finally organized an inaugural group consisting of herself, the jocular naturalist Ernest Thompson Seton, the droll R. B. Bennett, and the wickedly clever Dr. Frederick Banting.

However, this auspicious little gathering was forced to disband after its first meeting when it became immediately and painfully clear that nobody knew any quips.

"I've learned my lesson," Stephanie wrote ruefully to her trusted Toronto editor. "You simply cannot have a satisfactory gathering of literary lions without quips. The whole thing just dies a-borning – and a-boring! Ernie Thompson Seton told a long and complicated joke about a travelling salesman, a farmer's daughter, and a sandhill stag, that nobody got. Banting insisted on bringing the Islets of Langerhans into everything, and then became furious when Bennett woke up and asked him if he had any travel slides to go with his talk. I've never been so disappointed in my life. Of course, of that bunch, only Seton and I actually qualify as writers, and at that, Ernie signs everything he writes with a paw-print."

But disappointment was something to which Stephanie had long become accustomed. She continued undaunted in her literary pursuits, churning out an astounding number of humorous volumes, while continuing to keep her brother's literary output at a respectable level as well. However, as Stephen aged and as his health began to fail, Stephanie welcomed the lessening of her writing responsibilities. By the end of the 1930s, she was able to concentrate solely on her own work – a development that could not have come at a more convenient time for her, historically speaking.

With the advent of the Second World War, many male humorists either were called up for military service, or volunteered their talents to entertain troops abroad through stage-door canteens and travelling road-shows. Consequently, on the home front, nightclub stages were suddenly empty; the pages of publications like *Saturday Night* and *The New Yorker* were quickly devoid of humorous material; comical radio programs instantly had no writers, and publishers ran mad in the streets, searching in a panic for humorous collections to bring out in time for Christmas.

Alarming as the situation was, it could not have been more auspicious for female writers of humorous material, who really came into their own while the men were away. Photographs and newsreel footage of the times show hordes of laughing, eager young women, clad in kerchiefs and coveralls, filing into Hollywood studios' writers' buildings for their shifts.

Meanwhile, in publishing houses, similar overall-clad bevies of beauties received instruction in handling the cumbersome tools and heavy equipment heretofore strictly associated with male literary output. Now it was women who were taught to two-finger type, chew a pencil while thinking, and wad up and fire a discarded punch-line into a wastebasket at twenty paces, and they soon proved themselves as adept at these tasks as the absent menfolk.

For Stephanie, the war years turned out to be the bonanza of productivity that had been systematically denied to her all of her life. Her "Morning Chuckle" was syndicated in many North American newspapers by 1942; she did a brisk sideline in humorous sayings for the insatiable fortune-cookie industry; and those bygone girlhood days spent in dreamy perusal of *More Jokes for the John* proved invaluable now in helping her to develop merry quiddities of her own. In fact, it is Stephanie Leacock who is generally credited with the invention of the knock-knock joke.

But all good things, unfortunately, must come to an end,

and no sooner had Stephanie become accustomed to the endless work opportunities the war years afforded her, than
everything changed with the return of the men from the
front. All across North America, the story was the same:
Women who'd become happily used to the sense of accomplishment participation in the work force can bring were
suddenly told their labour was no longer required, and they
were politely invited to doff their coveralls in favour of their
long-discarded aprons.

Once more men were going to fill out the roster of Hollywood comedy writers. It was men who, once again, would
pen off-colour limericks as required, and men who would
bound, as of yore, onto nightclub stages to demand, "Hey,
anybody here from out of town?"

It is a tribute to Stephanie Leacock's stoicism that she did
not fight or rail against this new blow to her literary independence. She merely shrugged, turned over her "Morning
Chuckle" spot to a returning male war vet, and went her
way. And what way exactly, you ask, was that?

TWILIGHT OF A TROUPER

One thing for certain is that she did not go the way of count-
less other unemployed female humorists who, finding themselves in the same sad predicament, tried to carve out a
separate sphere for themselves by developing a new line of
humour, strictly feminine (although hardly feminist) in its
tone and context.

Since so many of the returning soldiers received housing
grants and other financial encouragement to settle down
and start families, the suburbs of North America began to
burgeon. This social development, in turn, made possible the
evolution of female domestic humour – those by-now-famil-
iar jaunty tales of young moms coping hilariously in the suburbs, with kids, hubby, and a large shaggy dog romping
through the pages of a volume entitled *Of Dust-Mice and
Milkmen* or some such thing.

But this kind of housecoated humour was not for the likes

of Stephanie Leacock. "I've worked too long and too hard to establish myself," she wrote to her editor friend, "to fritter it all away now with desperate jokes about bundt cakes, crabgrass, and the rinse cycle. Like the good shoemaker, I mean to stick to my last."

In an ideal world, Stephanie would have been able to see out her convictions. Stephen, her brother, had died in 1944, freeing her at last of the obligation of turning out his work as well as her own. She had an unlimited supply of creative energy, along with at least four hundred new knock-knock jokes at the ready. Unfortunately, this world is far from ideal. Times had changed, but social attitudes were no more in harmony with the cultivation of Stephanie's special talents than they ever had been.

In the early 1960s, an American television network approached Stephanie with the suggestion that she join a stable of writers engaged in turning out a situation comedy about a bunch of Beverly Hills socialites moving to the hill country of Arkansas. This offer was declined. About five years later, a radical feminist lesbian comic got in touch with Stephanie, inquiring as to whether Stephanie might be interested in writing material for her. Shocked, the sheltered Ontario spinster hung up in the comedienne's ear. In the mid-seventies, a textbook publisher involved in turning out pre-digested cram notes for slow students called on Stephanie to offer her the chance to write a simplified version of Stephen Leacock's *Elements of Political Science*. Needless to say, Stephanie slammed the door in his face.

After that, there were no more offers, of any kind. The old lady – and she *was* by now very old indeed – had no choice but to remain on in Orillia, continuing her writing and hunkering down in anticipation of a long dry spell before public tastes in humour shifted once more.

STEPHANIE LEACOCK TODAY

Yes, today. At the ripe old age of one hundred and eighteen, Stephanie Leacock is still very much a going concern, and still resident in Orillia, Ontario – where I discovered her when the trail of literary clues led inevitably to her front door.

She was pleased, but definitely not surprised, to welcome a stranger who had finally stumbled upon her existence. "I've waited for years for some Canadian humour buff to figure out who wrote Stevie's books for him," she told me briskly, wiping her hands on her apron. "Fortunately, Canadian humour buffs have always been in pretty short supply, so I assumed I was safe. However, now you're here, and I'd be a poor sport if I didn't ask you in and offer you a cup of tea and some fresh gingersnaps. Don't expect a merry twinkle from me, though. I always left that hokey stuff up to my brother."

That afternoon I spent with Stephanie Leacock in the parlour in Orillia is among the most delightful I have ever passed, anywhere. Stephanie's mind is as clear as ever, and she was more than willing to fill me in on what she's been up to for the last few years.

Still keen to keep up with her old interests, she edits a small economics newsletter called *The Calculator*. Recently, Orillia's local daily paper, *The Packet and Times*, offered a small subsidy to help Stephanie's work continue, and, in gratitude, she plans to rename her newsletter *The Packet-Calculator*.

Of course, the energy necessary to produce other writing has inevitably waned with the passage of time, but none of Stephanie's enthusiasm for current events has diminished, as demonstrated by her brisk and knowledgeable conversation on a number of themes.

On North American politics, for instance, she was both concise and acute: "Brian Mulroney and Ronald Reagan together provide the answer to that age-old question of where the snakes went after St. Patrick drove them out of Ireland. Besides," she went on to remark, "how can we trust two leaders who don't even pronounce their own names the way they're spelled?"

Speaking about women in politics, however, she makes

judgments no less stinging: "The signal accomplishment of Margaret Thatcher's tenure as Prime Minister is the way, through a kind of militant dowdiness, that she's managed to make the women of the Royal Family seem graceful and stylish by comparison. Take my word for it, it wasn't Princess Diana of Whatsis who perked up the image of that bunch, it was the dreary contrast of Maggie. And I assume that you realize that Mrs. Thatcher is actually Lord Kenneth Clark in a badly fitting wig."

Were she not so venerable, the old lady would seem truly scandalous indeed. I thoroughly enjoyed my time in Stephanie's company, however, and noted that there was one subject which caused even her to soften like a girl. I refer to the long-standing rivalry with her departed brother, Stephen.

"That man, it was all I could do not to throttle him," she confided to me, her customarily brusque manner concealing the real tenderness that she must have felt. "I couldn't stand him; I don't mind saying it. Why, when I asked him for a copy of *Sunshine Sketches* to give to a dear friend, he made me *buy* it from him, and not even at the author's discounted price! Buy it! A book that I had actually written. I forgave him a lot, but never that. Who can blame me?"

From a lesser woman, such a remark would have come out sounding cross-grained, but I assure you, on the lips of Stephanie Leacock, the subtext of sisterly affection shone right through. And when, with some hesitation, I explained to her that the article I intended to publish on the true authorship of Stephen Leacock's works would be greeted with scepticism in academic circles, at least initially, she seemed not only to understand at once, but to offer absolution.

"Oh sure. What else is new? Stephen's behind it some place, you can be sure of that. All of our lives, the same old story. Nothing but an endless string of honours accruing to him, while all I ever got was the fuzzy end of the lollipop. And now this. I swear I can hear that man laughing at me from beyond the grave."

Warm, vital, and playful – that is the quintessential Stephanie Leacock. How typical of her that her inevitable response would be to recollect the *leitmotif* of laughter that had always informed both her life and her brother's!

When I managed to tear myself reluctantly from the warm gingersnap-scented atmosphere of her congenial kitchen in Orillia, and headed out to the main road in the hopes of hitching a ride to the bus depot, I gave sober thought to the work that lay ahead of me – work, as I'd told Stephanie, that was unlikely to ever meet with one jot of sympathy or belief.

Somehow or other, though, I still managed to feel buoyed, whether by contact with the unquenchable spirit of the woman herself, or by virtue of the generous measure of Crown Royal Rye Whiskey she'd poured into the cup of tea she served me, I couldn't really say.

For whatever reason, I felt girded and prepared for the labour that lay ahead, the labour whose fruits I have spread before you in this publication. If one credulous soul among you credits what I have written here about Stephanie Leacock, then neither Stephanie's struggle, nor my own attempts to document it, will have been in vain.

The Stream of Consciousness-Raising

It was the Museum of Man debate that caused all the trouble in the group. Although the argument could have been about anything, like combat roles for women in the military, or. . . .

I'd better start by telling you something about the group, which is (was?) pretty special in its way: the oldest established floating female consciousness-raising group north of New York. Oh, I suppose "consciousness-raising" sounds desperately old-hat, with its connotations of earnest dames in dashikis, cross-legged in a circle on the rug in somebody's living-room, their centre-parted heads bobbing in agreement over some point of oppression, and their dangling earrings jingling corroboration.

Maybe our group *was* a bit like that in the beginning. Back in the late sixties, when we were all single and lived in studio apartments, which we took turns volunteering as locations for the meetings, along with a bag of rancid ripple chips and some Mogen David wine.

By the seventies, most of us were living with men who took turns being turfed out of the apartment – a one-bedroom by now – depending on whose place had been commandeered for the meeting. All of us were now responsible for refreshments, and we each brought a dish. The dish was lasagna.

Even as the decade gave way to the eighties, the weekly meetings showed no signs of petering out. Although we'd all been through some changes. Mostly gustatory. There was the herbal-tea-and-rice-cracker phase, satay suppers, a brief flirtation with cheese trays, and one particularly dark period in 1981 when all we could jointly stomach was vodka martinis straight up with a twist.

I should also mention that we were all renting the ground floor of houses by now, strewn with diaper pails and defaced by Jolly Jumper hooks – although the men who'd occasioned the kids and had vacated for our meetings in the seventies had long since taken a hike of a far more permanent kind.

But through all the changes, the group held firm and the meetings persisted with the weekly predictability of *TV Guide*. Until the Museum of Man loomed up, like the tip of some hulking ideological iceberg.

"Typical, typical," Mary Ellen declared, jabbing with her fork at the vast mountain of tortellini she'd ordered, instead of the little salad she'd promised herself. Since the group had started meeting in restaurants in the mid-eighties, not only were we eating higher on the hog, we were eating more of it. "Museum of *Man*. As if history was all about *them*."

"It *is*," Leslie pointed out gently. "But changing the name to Museum of Humanity would be a step in the right direction. What woman in her right mind thinks of herself as 'Man'?"

"I do sometimes," I heard myself announce unexpectedly. "Not as a *man*, but I like the idea of being part of Mankind. Then equality doesn't seem so far away."

The group simultaneously dropped their forks in astonishment, abandoning the lamb shaslik, vol-au-vent, and veal piccata they had all ordered instead of a little salad. Only Melissa spoke up to defend me.

"I know what you mean. Somehow, the distaff side is the dull one, and trying to glamourize it makes it even worse. Like the idea of salaries for homemakers. Ugh. They start paying us to do that and we'll never get out of the kitchen."

"You're totally colonized," Leslie exclaimed, "the pair of you. There's nothing wrong with housework, except that women do it."

"Maybe so," I said, "but you notice how few men are lining up to stay home and take care of the kids? Even in the States, where Congress has given them the right to a leave of absence? Instinctively they know. No homemaker of either sex is going to make it onto the cover of *Fortune* magazine."

Mary Ellen was angry enough to start tearing her napkin into tiny shreds – a cloth napkin, at that. "Your value system is so male it makes me sick. Next thing you'll be telling me the Sistine ceiling is a higher achievement than the tapestries woven by anonymous women."

I didn't tell her that, but Melissa did. Before you knew it, all of us had shredded our napkins and risen in a frozen huff – and the oldest established floating female consciousness-raising group north of New York was no more.

We'd come a cropper – like every women's group before us – over the Big One: Namely, does equality consist of getting what men have got, or in carving out some separate sphere with entirely new criteria of what constitutes prestige and accomplishment?

It's a conundrum unlikely to be solved in our lifetime, of course. Meanwhile, as proximate cause of all the trouble, I'd like to take the responsibility of getting the group back together for a reconciliatory meeting. Maybe a nice outing to some place non-controversial. Like the "Giant Step for Mankind" exhibit at the space-technology museum. Or the production of *Man of La Mancha* playing down in the theatre district. Or . . . on second thought, maybe I'll just let well enough alone, and concentrate on working the effect of all those little salads off my waistline.

THE
MAN
MANUAL

Nowadays, no savvy consumer would dream of making a decision as important as buying a car without first consulting the appropriate guidebooks. Since I am, I like to think, as savvy as the next consumer, I've spent a considerable amount of time over the past few weeks poring over car manuals, auto test results, and back issues of *Consumer Reports*. And while I am no farther ahead in knowing which vehicle is right for me, I have at least managed to make one collateral – and arguably far more important – decision: If there are manuals on the market to assist in picking out a mere automobile, there should also be manuals to aid in the infinitely trickier task of choosing a relationship.

The Man Manual, they could call it. Or *Womanual*, if the

desired date happens to be with a female. But from my own point of view, the more urgent priority is the man manual, and to facilitate its publication, I have taken the liberty of roughing out the first few chapters. See what you think.

Chapter One: Making That Basic Choice. Before you focus on the specifics of any individual man, you must first make a primary decision crucial to any permanent relationship. The question to ask yourself is: "Should I take a chance on a used model?"

Often referred to as "previously loved", the second-hand man can be either merely used, or entirely used up. To determine which, try to ascertain exactly how much mileage he has on him. The best way to find out is by obtaining his history of previous partnerships.

Does he seem to have changed hands many times, been frequently but inadequately serviced, or traded too often and without satisfactory explanation? If so, avoid, avoid.

On the other hand, if he has enjoyed a trouble-free association with one or two previous partners, and seems only moderately driven, there is little reason to bypass him in favour of a man with no history at all on the highway of life.

Chapter Two: Choosing The Model That's Right For You. Whichever way you decide to take the auto-emotive plunge, there are a number of secondary choices to be made when selecting a man to meet your particular needs. Ask yourself the following:

1) *How important is automatic transmission?* For those inexperienced in relationships, very. Men are traditionally non-communicative creatures, and one equipped only with standard transmission will convey precious few of his thoughts to you. But automatic transmission indicates that he is the type who will always communicate his inner feelings openly, easily, and as a matter of course.

2) *Do I go convertible or hardtop?* Again, look at your own needs before deciding. A convertible man is willing to alter his opinions, adapts easily to new circumstances, and can be broken of bad habits – like compulsive throat-clearing – with a minimum of effort. The hardtop man, as his name implies, is inflexible from the neck up and between the ears.

3) *Should I choose front-wheel drive, and what is it?* Possibly, and let me explain what it is. A front-wheel-driven man is dominated by mental thrust, and therefore propelled by his intellect. The rear-wheel man, conversely, finds his centre of drive somewhere, uh, lower on his chassis, and – well, I think you get the idea. Your choice really depends on whether you like the cerebral sort, or if you prefer the kind of guy who takes a load off his mind by standing up.

Chapter Three: A Glossary of Options. Novices are often puzzled by terminology when it comes to choosing options in relationships, so let's deal with some of the more confusing terms:

1) *Cruise control.* The degree to which a man is able to refrain from checking out other women when he's in your company.

2) *Heavy-duty suspension.* A definite must, if you require total and unquestioning trust from your mate. Men equipped with this option can be counted on to suspend disbelief, even in the most suspicious of circumstances – as when you return home at four in the morning from a reconciliatory lunch with your old boyfriend.

3) *Electric antenna.* His level of sensitivity to your alterations of mood, and his ability to detect volatile troublespots in the atmosphere of your relationship.

4) *Four on the floor.* An option you *don't* want, unless you like spending your time with a man who can often be found on his hands and knees, blind drunk.

So, there you have it, at least in embryo. The first few tantalizing chapters of *The Man Manual.* How do you feel about it so far? I want you to be totally honest, now.

What do you think about an initial print run of, oh, let's say two hundred thousand, timed to come out for the Christmas buying season? Followed by a half-million in paperback geared to the summertime beach crowd? Yeah. I think so too. A half a million paperback, at the very least.

ROSES ARE RED

Every Valentine's Day in this country, a vivid little drama is played out. No, I'm not talking about the upbeat romantic comedy of young lovers exchanging tokens of the holiday. Nor do I refer to the *Sturm und Drang* tragedy that occurs in the kitchens of the married when somebody has forgotten to buy a Valentine's gift.

I mean the infinitely more high-pitched conflict that rages between two female housemates when one of them gets a valentine from an admirer and the other does not.

Because it's such a classic drama, it seems to me that by now we really should *make* it a classic, by getting it down on paper, once and for all, in a really definitive form. As usual, it appears that this task has devolved upon me, and so I dutifully embrace it. Here, then, is the play for all seasons that shall endure as long as expensive downtown houses are for rent and as long as there are women-between-men who decide to rent them. The curtain rises on:

ROSES ARE RED; A PLAY FOR ST. VALENTINE'S DAY.

Time: The present. *Place*: The Formica-and-white-pine kitchen of a renovated house in a pleasant downtown area of a large city. *Characters*: Nina and her housemate, Rose. Both pleasant-looking women in their middle thirties.
> (*As the curtain rises,* NINA, *in a bathrobe, is busily buttering toast and making coffee. Occasionally she glances out the window as if expecting someone. But as* ROSE *enters, bathrobe-clad and scuffing in her slippers,* NINA *quickly absorbs herself in buttering.*)

ROSE (*yawns*): Morning.

NINA (*eagerly*): So?

ROSE: So? What do you mean, "so"? (*As* NINA *says nothing*) Nina, I walk into the kitchen on Valentine's Day – always a touchy one for the terminally single – and your first word of the day to me is "so"?

NINA: So?

ROSE: No wonder your last housemate left in a huff. (*She sits.*)

NINA: She did not leave in a huff, Rose. She left in a Honda Civic. *My* Honda Civic. With a train case full of my jewellery, towels, and stock certificates. So far the police haven't turned up a single lead.

ROSE: Well, I can guess what drove her to kleptomania. What is this "so" business supposed to mean?

NINA: So how was it last night? Your date?

ROSE: Oh, that. Another clunker. On Valentine's Eve, yet. Although I suppose it figures.

NINA (*brightly*): A clunker?

ROSE: Yes. Can you make an effort to sound less delighted?

NINA: Rose, you're the only single friend I have left, and the rent on this house is twelve hundred a month. When *you* go –

ROSE: I'm not going anywhere, believe me. Is that coffee? (*She gets up, pours herself a cup.*) Want some?

NINA: Sure. (*As* ROSE *pours*) That bad, eh? (*Stirring sugar into her cup*) What was he, short?

ROSE (*pouring cream*): Worse than short.

NINA: What could be worse than short? Don't put away the cream.

ROSE (*hands her the cream*): A man whose nose is so upturned that if he let a smile be his umbrella, he'd drown. Plus which, he had a pinkie ring and a blinking dog in the car's rear window. Should I go on?

NINA: Go on.

ROSE (*going on*): He referred to sex on a first date as a "viable option".

NINA (*sympathetically, as she puts the cream in the fridge*): Oh, Rose . . .

> (*Suddenly, off-stage, there is the chime of the front door-bell.*)

ROSE: Now, who could . . . ?

NINA (*quickly*): I'll get it.

> (*She tightens the belt on her bathrobe and hurriedly exits.* ROSE, *meanwhile, sips her coffee meditatively. Quickly* NINA *returns. In her arms, wrapped up with a bow, is a long florist's box.*)

NINA (*breathless with excitement*): Well, well. Guess whose Valentine's Day has just been redeemed! (*Thrusts the box at* ROSE.)

ROSE (*bewildered*): What . . . ? (*In a daze, she opens the box, pulls out a rose.*)

NINA: Roses. I knew it. A bunch of roses long enough to choke a giraffe. And a card? Is there a card?

ROSE (*locating the card*): Yes. (*Hands it to* NINA.) You read it. My glasses are upstairs.

NINA (*reads the envelope*): "To the fairest Rose of them all."

ROSE: For me?

NINA (*drily*): Yes, Rose, I would imagine so. No one gives roses to girls named Nina. Girls named Nina get chafing-dishes. Do you want me to open the card?

ROSE (*stunned*): Sure, I guess. . . .

(*NINA rips the envelope open and reads the card to herself.*)

ROSE: Well?

NINA: It's lovely. (*Reads*) "Some roses are red, but my Rose is best. Sweet and sexy and beauty-blest."

ROSE: My God, what a lyric.

NINA: What would you prefer? "Viable option"? (*Bitterly*) Oh, Rose, I knew it. (*Flings the card down.*) You've met someone.

ROSE (*ducks down to retrieve the card*): No, I haven't, I swear. (*Hands the card to NINA.*) Is there more? What does the rest of it say?

NINA (*reads*): "From someone who can't forget that night at the Hilton, and wants to claim all the nights to come." (*Pause*) What did I tell you? You're as good as out the door.

ROSE: Nina, I haven't got the faintest idea who this is.

NINA: My God, how many unforgettable nights at the Hilton have you handed *out*? Anyway, no need to cudgel your brains. He'll be along to claim his prize soon enough, I'm sure. Moving in with me does it every time, you know. Chronically dateless women cross this threshold, women who haven't been out with a guy since the Senior Prom. They move in here and – bingo! Their life changes in the twinkling of an eye.

ROSE: Will you shut up? It's roses and an anonymous card. That is *it*. I'll probably never even know who sent them.

NINA (*on a roll*): Four times already this year, Rose. Four times. Count 'em. Four times it's happened. Four housemates in a row, not counting the kleptomaniac, who swore to me they would remain unattached, not only as a gesture of solidarity with me, but as a pre-condition of signing the lease. And yet, in a matter of weeks, each one in succession met and married a tall, tender, witty, and compassionate quantum physicist who composed brilliant poetry on the side.

ROSE: That lets me out. This guy's poetry sucks.

NINA: Who is he, Rose? I might as well know. So I can refer to him by name at the wedding ceremony.

ROSE (*irritably*): I'm telling you, I haven't a clue. . . . (*Feverishly*) Hilton, Hilton. . . . Did I stay at the Hilton in Montreal?

NINA: Aha!

ROSE: Naw, couldn't be. The one guy I met in Montreal kept saying, "C'est la gare. That's the railway station. Ha ha." Please, God, don't let it be him.

NINA (*dolefully, beginning to gather up breakfast things*): Why is it that everybody else's life moves forward, while mine just stagnates in one spot? I never meet anybody. Meanwhile, my friends meet guys, break up with guys, move in with new guys, marry yet *other* guys, raise their kids, flirt with lesbianism, and finally settle down with guys they haven't seen since Grade Three. I meanwhile feel overbooked if, in the same space of time, I've acquired a new pair of shoes.

ROSE (*becoming frantic, as she arranges the roses in a vase*): Ah! What about the annual meeting in Vancouver last year? *That* guy was cute, and wasn't he the one who could do that trick with a glass, a toothpick, and a pound of raisins? (*Pause, then discouraged*) Naw. That was the Hotel Vancouver. And anyway, that guy turned out to be married.

NINA: It's no use trying to spare me, Rose. You've met Mr. Right, and can't bring yourself to break it to me.

ROSE (*snatching up the card and squinting at it shortsightedly*): Nina, you've got to shut up and let me think. "That night at the Hilton . . ." Hey, that package deal in Cancún! Was *that* a Hilton? (*Pause*) I doubt it. Not when the towels say "Brooklyn YMCA". Anyway, *that* was the guy who turned up in my room at two a.m. in lederhosen with a suitcase full of block and tackle . . . (*Shudders at the memory*) Oh, Nina, I've had a horrible life!

(*The phone on the wall rings.*)

NINA (*goes for it*): I'll get it.

ROSE (*faster, intercepting her*): No way. This better be him, whoever he – Hello? (*Pause*) No, but . . . (*Pause*) Oh, I see. (*Pause, glances at* NINA.) Thanks, I will. Bye.

(ROSE *cradles the phone, then looks at* NINA *angrily.*)

NINA (*tentatively*): So?

ROSE (*suppressing wrath*): "So" seems to be your word for the day, doesn't it?

NINA (*nervously*): What's the matter? Was it him?

ROSE: It was the flower shop. (*Meaningfully*) Brigham's Flowers.

NINA (*in a small, subdued voice*): Oh.

ROSE: The same Brigham's Flowers where these roses came from.

NINA: Oh.

ROSE: Yes, "oh". What's that, your new word for the day? (*As NINA says nothing*) It seems you forgot your credit card there when you paid for the flowers, Nina.

NINA (*startled*): My – ? Oh, my God. Did I?

ROSE: Yes. And wasn't it nice of them to call? (*Rising anger*) Otherwise I would have gone through every sordid, depressing, and pointless out-of-town encounter I've ever had, trying to figure out who in the hell –

NINA (*backing away*): Rose, please don't be mad.

ROSE (*flinging the roses, one by one to the floor*): Mad? Why on earth would you do such a thing to me? On Valentine's Day, of all days! (*Advances on her, angrily.*)

NINA (*holding up a chair to protect herself*): That's – that's *why* I did it, Rose!

ROSE (*stops*): What?

NINA (*beginning to cry*): Be – because it's Valentine's Day, and you told me how much it means to you. And how depressed you get if no one sends you a box of candy, or a card, or –

ROSE: Or some flowers. (*Pause, then begins picking up the roses from the floor.*) Yes, I did say that. But Nina, this is hardly the answer!

NINA (*still sniffling*): I didn't know I'd forgotten my credit card. I had no idea they'd phone. . . .

ROSE: No, I suppose not.

NINA: I wanted it to be a – little dash of mystery and romance in your day. I'm sorry, Rose.

ROSE (*rearranging the flowers in the vase*): This huge bunch of long-stemmed roses. Forty bucks' worth, at least.

NINA (*wipes her nose on her sleeve*): Fifty-two-sixty. Counting tax.

ROSE: And this card ... "Some roses are red, But my Rose is best"?

NINA: It took me a long time to come up with something that terrible.

ROSE (*laughs*): I'll bet. And that Academy Award-winning performance you turned in as the paranoid friend.

NINA: Oh, that part was easy. I've had lots of practice.

ROSE: Nina, you are nuts.

NINA: I meant well. I really did. And you're the best housemate I've ever had.

ROSE: Only because I can't find a man, and there's nothing in the place worth stealing.

NINA: No. I mean that you deserve a valentine, Rose. Even if it's only from me.

ROSE (*hugs her*): They're beautiful flowers, Nina. You're an idiot and the card is a disgrace, but your taste in flowers is topnotch.

NINA: Next year, they'll be from a man. Trust me. You want to expand your social life, move in with Nina.

ROSE: Shut up, Nina.

NINA: Happy Valentine's Day, Rose. Uh ... what did that guy plan to *do* with that block and tackle?

ROSE: Shut up, Nina.

NINA: Happy Valentine's Day, Rose.

(*And the curtain falls.*)

HOW-TO VIDEOS

If I complain about video cassettes, I don't want you to leap to the automatic conclusion that I am refusing to move with the times. I have no problem with the times. In fact, thanks to the times, my life comes equipped with a host of exciting standard features that, only a few short years ago, would have seemed not only implausible, but sinfully exotic into the bargain.

My electronic typewriter, for example. To the uninitiated, the subtle distinction between this and an ordinary electric typewriter might be difficult to grasp. But an electronic typewriter costs more. When the man in the store told me exactly how *much* more, I let out a cry of admiration for the marvels of technology and steadied myself against the near-

114

est Olympia ES 80, which he immediately insisted that I buy. Once he'd opened the thing up, my admiration was in no way diminished by noting that there were virtually no works inside. Imagine a brand-new typewriter that offers you half as much equipment at twice the price, and yet somehow manages to weigh more than a dead Charolais. And did I remember to mention that after one time through, you get to throw the ribbon away?

I feel similarly privileged to be alive in the age of dental plaque – a condition of which nothing had been heard prior to 1982, and of which the lack was not felt until well into 1984. Today, of course, it's plaque this and plaque that, and even if your teeth continue to fall out of your head at the same rate as in those bad old pre-plaque days, at least now there is something to blame.

So you see that it's not a generalized complaint I'm lodging against the manifestations of modernity, but a very specific assault on video cassettes. Most particularly, in case you haven't already guessed, how-to video cassettes.

Surely you've seen them. Raquel Welch, her hair full of gel and her eyes full of missionary intent, stepping onto the video screen to lead us, even more unctuously than Jane Fonda, in a workout. Craig Claiborne caught in the act of deboning, like some malevolent Hitchcock son disposing of a relative with the precision of a surgeon and the conscience of a Dade County realtor.

And now that something called Video Data Service of Roanoke, Virginia, is on the scene, the worst has happened. They offer a video tape to teach your parrot how to talk.

Although apprehensive when I first heard tell of the parrot cassette, I was sufficiently curious to invest. What I brought home was a tape featuring real pollies reciting for twelve-minute stretches such essentials of parrot parlay as "I love you," and "I'm a green chicken."

Well. This seemingly harmless exposure to educational programming had disastrous results indeed. Not only did my parrot become hopelessly addicted to the repetitive nature of the material it was ingesting (the technical term for this condition is *parrotinitis*), but it began demanding, in raucous tones, more and more television fare tailored to its tastes. "Rona Parrot's Hollywood" found its way into our home. Then a rock video by the nihilistic group Dead Parrot. On the positive side of the ledger, at least the French classic film *Les Enfants du Parrotdis* became required viewing once or twice a week.

But much worse even than that ensued when video cassettes entered the lives of my pet fish. Along with the tank had come an innocent-looking how-to video entitled "Outfitting Your Aquarium". At first, when I played it, I thought it cute that all the inhabitants of the tank came swimming over to press their noses (if fish can be said to have noses) against the glass to watch the show. But then the goldfish began to be obviously affected, and started exhibiting alarmingly materialistic tendencies. They wanted everything they saw on the screen, including the little plaster diver opening the treasure chest, and the scale model replica of Neuschwanstein.

The snails were next. They soon tired of watching "Outfitting an Aquarium", claiming that it moved too fast for them, and began clamouring for *Masterpiece Theatre*, mainly because they had discovered in Alistair Cooke someone who spoke slowly and distinctly enough for them to keep up.

Not surprisingly, the angel-fish moved on from the video cassette to a fascination for the religious cable channel; the neon fish suddenly could talk of nothing but Broadway, and the kissing gouramis graduated to hard porn.

But perhaps the worst casualties of all were the guppies. Thanks to television, the guppies learned they were members of a trendy demographic group called Generationally Urban Pets, known familiarly as GUPpies. After that, there was no dealing with them. All they were interested in watching on television any more, apart from the Craig Claiborne video, was *Moonlighting* and *Cheers*. Soon they demanded that the tank be refilled with Perrier. And it was, I confess, with more than a fugitive tear that I finally acceded to their pressure to replace the plaster diver in the tank with a little cost accountant in a Brooks Brothers suit.

A Day
at the
Opera

I'm sure you're as sick as I am of hearing that the age of operatic tragedy is past, and how minimal are the possibilities of high drama in the banal world we inhabit. That's why I was delighted to tune in to the weekly Metropolitan Opera radio broadcast a few Saturdays ago, and discover Imbroglio's modern masterpiece, *I Yuppi*.

The action is set in a mythical northern city called Taranto or Toronno or something like that (the whole thing's in Italian, of course, so the names were a bit difficult to catch); and the protagonists are lovers named Kyle and Astrid. (At least I *think* those were the names. As I say, everything goes by pretty fast in a foreign language.)

Anyway, when the story opens, Kyle and Astrid, although not married, are living together. This may sound unusual for an opera, but as Astrid explains in her opening aria, she feels deep ambivalence about the concept of commitment, while Kyle's therapist has definitely advised against any "pressure toward bonding", at least until Kyle manages to resolve his long-standing conflict around rental tuxes.

By the time the female chorus arrives, dressed in sweatsuits and Adidas (did I remember to explain that Act One is set in the juice bar at Astrid's fitness club?), it is clear that Astrid is unhappy because of Kyle's insistence that they take two weeks in February to scuba on Cozumel, even though he knows very well that's the one time of the year Astrid cannot possibly get away from the small brokerage firm that she runs.

When Kyle makes his impressive entrance in the Rabbit to pick up Astrid from the fitness club (her Audi is in for an oil change), she attempts to confront him by suggesting that it's his unconscious resentment of her success in business that has prompted his desire to take holidays at an inconvenient juncture.

But Kyle refutes this, in one of the most moving tenor arias of the modern repertoire, "Cara, partite ma cassa" ("Honey, get off my case") as the curtain falls on Act One of *I Yuppi*.

The intermission feature was equally riveting – a lecture by a prominent musicologist that helped to put the works of Emilio Imbroglio into perspective. As the expert explained, *I Yuppi* follows in a tradition of opera established by Imbroglio back in the sixties, with his first work, which was set in the courtroom of the Chicago Eight conspiracy trial, and was called *The Tales of Abby Hoffman*.

But times and musical tastes changed, so that the seventies found Imbroglio grappling with consumerism as a basis for conflict in his works, most notably *Madama Batterfry*, his first examination of the tragic potential of food. This triumph was followed by two works of automotive angst, *Car Men* and *The Cadillac of Seville*, which, while less successful, indisputably set the stage for Imbroglio's eighties masterwork, *I Yuppi*.

Armed with this useful background information, I was better able to understand and enjoy Act Two of *I Yuppi*, which opens with a lyrical duet between Astrid and Kyle, who have decided to be mature about their differences by planning separate vacations. Seated in their broadloomed living-room amidst a welter of holiday brochures, they sing "Io ho riservazioni" ("I've got reservations") which concerns the relative merits of French-immersion ski seminars in the Alps, a computer camp in Belize, and a Tahitian tennis compound.

But this light-hearted moment is short-lived, for suddenly their lawyer is on the phone with sobering news about the renegotiation of their mortgage. Then the doorbell rings, and the entire Neighbourhood Residents' Association enters to announce that City Hall has sided with a developer who plans to build a bikers' video arcade right across the street.

This double volley of woe is too much for Astrid. In a trance, she rises, goes into her handsomely appointed kitchen complete with solid-pine butcher's block, and begins methodically feeding vacation literature into the Osterizer.

She has, as Kyle and the chorus rapidly realize, gone mad. The Neighbourhood Residents' Association begins offering Kyle therapists' home numbers as well as discordant and contradictory suggestions on how to repair the Osterizer, but Kyle will hear none of it. Defiantly, he snatches up his Morlands sheepskin jacket and heads out to the specialty food shop, to drown his sorrows in chèvre. The curtain falls.

Well, I won't spoil *I Yuppi* for you by telling you how Act Three comes out. Suffice it to say that Astrid's cross-dressing brother, played by a mezzo-soprano in a *travesti* role, turns up to reveal a family secret which, along with a phone call from the mechanic who has startling news about the Audi, provides Kyle and Astrid with an opportunity for spiritual salvation.

I think I've told you enough to give you the general idea. Not only does Emilio Imbroglio's *I Yuppi* speak movingly and poignantly to today's troubled generation, it also furnishes proof positive that opera has lost none of its relevance in a world racked by the plethora of moral choices that abundance brings.

Best of all, it's available on record, cassette, and compact disc.

BI-

URBANISM

When you've been in the social-prognostication game as long as I have, (i.e., just long enough to have learned how to spell "prognostication"), you get used to being ahead of your time. No sooner do I sense the incipient glint of an upcoming trend beginning to creep over the anthropological horizon like rosy-fingered dawn than – presto – some social scientist or stringer for *People* magazine declares it a full-blown fad.

For instance, it wasn't too long ago that I doodled a quick marginal note to myself about the increasing fashionability of dual-city dwelling. You know the sort of people involved: Show-biz people who live here but also sublet inadequately fumigated utility closets in lower Manhattan for approximately the same sum required to amortize the national debt

of Mexico. Footloose business folk into something called "consulting" – which means they get first-named at airports and cost more to lunch with than Sydney Biddle Barrows. And, of course, courting couples who have discovered that the longevity of the romance is directly proportional to the number of miles you keep between your apartment and that of your beloved.

To cover all of these late-twentieth-century rewrites of *A Tale of Two Cities*, what struck me as the right term was *bi-urbanism*. So I jotted that down too, along with a stern injunction to myself to develop this flimsy social observation into an unnecessarily elaborate thesis at the first available opportunity.

Well, wouldn't you know it? Someone has beaten me to the punch again. A gang of someones. A gang of *sociologists*, to put it as bluntly as I can and still hope to see my work appear in mainstream bookstores. The sociologists are planning to hold a Symposium on Bi-Urbanism, and have already sent out the calendar of events. A copy of this document showed up in my mailbox yesterday, along with the usual abject letter from Richard Gere begging me to reconsider, and some discount coupons for Three-in-One oil.

On the basis of a fast perusal of the symposium brochure, I'd have to say that the sociologists have the subject pretty much covered. One of the main lectures will be "Bi-Urbanism Means Always Having to Say You're Sorry", and details the problems of always missing important phone calls, tax audits, and weddings (including your own) because these events invariably go on in the home city where you are *not*.

"No matter where the bi-urbanist is, he is out of town," the brochure reports, and says the lecturer will demonstrate that, while wild parties only occur in Town A while you are in Town B, liquor strikes, transit strikes, power failures, and papal visits can always be counted on to afflict the city you are about to arrive in.

"A Bi-Urbanist's Day" is another lecture being offered, featuring an hour-by-hour breakdown (in both senses of the word) of a typical day endured by anyone foolhardy enough to run his life in two different places.

"7 a.m. Down to the station in City A to catch the early-morning express train to City B, where you are expected later in the morning.

"9 a.m. Sit fuming in the waiting-room as the railway offers endless and often contradictory excuses for why the train still hasn't left.

"10 a.m. Miss the train because you are on the phone warning your colleagues in City B that you will be arriving three hours late.

"12 p.m. Lunch-time on the airplane, which it has cost you $87.50 plus $44.92 in cab fare to catch. Congratulate yourself that you have at least missed the Interurban Snack of funny grey roast beef and a dessert that tastes like an Avon product, which they will be serving right now on the train.

"12:01 p.m. Cease congratulating yourself as the flight attendant comes by with the Interurban Snack of funny pink chicken and a dessert that tastes like an Alberto-Culver product."

Eventually, of course, the weary bi-urbanist will make his way to his other abode in City B, around about one in the morning – only to discover that there is no: wine, Aspirin, up-to-date TV schedule, milk for morning coffee, or oregano. Therefore, another useful aspect of the sociologists' bi-urbanism symposium will be the workshops they are offering on how to cope with the kind of city-straddling problems outlined above.

"How to Wake Up and Know Instantly Where You Are" promises to suggest ways to avoid the inevitable confusion constant city-hopping can generate. "Make sure the phone in your second home is a different colour," the pundits advise. "That way, you'll recall which town you were in when you accepted Jerry's invitation to lunch. Keep separate appointment books so you know *which* Jerry it is you are lunching with. Failing that, simply lunch with everyone named Jerry you know in both of your cities of residence."

For my money, though, the most indispensable of all the bi-urbanism workshops is bound to be "Walk Softly and Carry a Big Bag", which will enumerate exactly what items the well-prepared bi-urbanist must carry on his person at all times, irrespective of which city he is in. A clothesbrush, of course. Running shoes, by all means. Both appointment books, subway tokens in the currency of both home towns, Aspirin, a jar of non-dairy creamer. Oh yes – and a tin of oregano.

As the sociologists tell us, no matter which town you are in, you never know when you'll get the urge for a late-night snack of spaghetti bolognese.

Damage Control
in the Ancient World

Immersed in media stories of presidential misconduct and covert ministerial wrongdoing, we tend to think of the term "damage control" as a phenomenon of fairly recent vintage. We forget that as long as there have been governments, there have also been governmental transgressions, secret operations, and the need to contain their ravages – which means that the concept of damage control has been an integral aspect of human interaction from the very dawn of recorded time. And probably for some time before that.

Consider, if you will, the illustrative example of the Amazons. Little is know of these women, except that, according to Greek mythology, they were a tribe of female warriors from Scythia, and were tricky gals to date. As legend had it, not only did the Amazons have the disconcerting habit of

124

lopping off one breast in order to improve their aim in archery, they were also notoriously negative about men as a group. This was demonstrated by the fact that these women kept their lovers in cages, letting them out only to provide a diversion in the boudoir, and then immediately locked them up again, once the fun was over.

Perhaps the striking absence of boy-craziness among the Amazons stemmed from the fact that Hercules had once slain their queen, Hippolyta, in order to accomplish the last of his nine labours, by obtaining her belt. Women, as we know, have a singular way of holding grudges, particularly when articles of clothing are involved.

But in any case and for whatever reason, the Amazons set themselves up as a matriarchy, and posted signs all over the queendom that read: "No Boys Allowed. This Means You, Buster", "The Only Good Male Is Air Mail", and "No Flies on Us, or on Our Pants".

How were the Amazons for so long able to get away with this matriarchal domination of all the men in the immediate Scythian area? Simple. Since biology was not a required course in those days, nobody had yet realized that reproduction had anything to do with men. Women got all the credit for the production of children, and the Amazons exploited that fact to keep the men down. Even when it started to become evident to women that there was a direct connection between copulation and procreation, they shrewdly chose to keep this information to themselves, instinctively aware that such volatile news in the wrong hands could spell disaster for the entire matriarchal system.

However, as we know, the facts about paternity eventually became too hot to either handle or suppress. Can you imagine the scene of consternation amongst the Amazonian leaders the day the bad news leaked out?

If not, let me take you back in time to that fateful afternoon in ancient Scythia. We are in the boardroom of the palace of the Queen of the Amazons, where the Queen herself is in an emergency huddle with several of her top staff advisers. The crest over her throne bears the inscribed motto: "One Breast Good, Two Breasts Bad".

QUEEN: Seriously, though, is this a problem? I'm sorry, ladies, I just don't accept that this has to be such a major problem.

CHIEF ADVISER (sighs): Let me run it by you one more time, Your Majesty. They're on to us. The guys have figured out the score. About scoring. You know, the procreation thing? They're beginning to suspect where babies come from, and that we girls don't do it all by ourselves after all.

QUEEN: You're kidding. Who says we don't?

PROPAGANDA MINISTER: There's no point continuing to stonewall on this, Your Majesty. Definitely, they're on to us.

QUEEN: Who let it out?

PRESS SECRETARY: It's not a question of *who*, Your Majesty. No one specifically slipped up. It was only a matter of time, really, before they put two and two together. You know ... "Hi, handsome, I'm having you sent to my tent after the battle." Then, hug and kiss and so on and so on ... And bingo. Nine months later, the proverbial bouncing bundle. How long were we going to keep on taking them in with that coincidence, like a rabbit pulled out of thin air?

QUEEN (with a nostalgic sigh): Gosh, it was fun while it lasted, though, wasn't it?

CHIEF ADVISER: I say there's still a way to contain it.

PROPAGANDA MINISTER: Forget it.

CHIEF ADVISER: No, hear me out. So far, what have we got? Just a bunch of male science journalists making allegations in the popular press.

PROPAGANDA MINISTER: Fairly substantive allegations, unfortunately. I mean, this "spam" or "sperm" idea of theirs is pretty hard to refute. Deep down, we have to admit they're right.

CHIEF ADVISER: That's just where we'll keep it. Deep down.

PROPAGANDA MINISTER: Well, maybe there's a way at that. .... The trick is to feed them something, but not too much. Making it *look* like we're making a clean breast of – er, that is ... (Glances anxiously up at the crest.)

CHIEF ADVISER: Never mind. We get the point. How be we issue a statement along these lines: "In response to rumours that males sire babies, a judicial inquiry will be launched by the Queen to – "

QUEEN: Judicial inquiry? No way. Forget that. That's far too much. I mean, do you really relish the idea of every woman in pagandom humiliated by a succession of old boyfriends getting up on the stand to reminisce about their romantic adventures? "That's right, your honour. I have it right here in my diary. My tryst with the Propaganda Minister was on April 4 last. And then, just this past December, the Propaganda Minister gave birth to – "

PROPAGANDA MINISTER (*hastily*): You may be right, Your Majesty. A judicial inquiry could be embarrassing.

CHIEF ADVISER: Then let's go the modified hang-out route on this thing.

QUEEN: The what? It sounds like what those dirty old men do, down in the Arcadian grove.

CHIEF ADVISER: What I'm saying is, it was a tactical mistake, right in the beginning when this thing first surfaced, *not* to come back with some kind of statement to mollify the men. I said that, if you'll recall, right at the outset.

PROPAGANDA MINISTER: No, I do not recall that. What I *do* recall you saying was, "Oh God, does this mean his relatives will buy the kid a drum for his birthday?"

CHIEF ADVISER: Let's not dwell on ancient history.

QUEEN: But this *is* ancient history.

CHIEF ADVISER: All I'm suggesting is that there were ways of containing the spill. And maybe even now it's not too late. For example, suppose the Press Secretary here reads a nice contrite-sounding little statement. Something to the effect of: "Allegations that males are involved in the conception process are emphatically denied by the palace. However, the Queen would like to take this opportunity to give full credit to the male of the species for putting women in the *mood* to conceive." Well, that's rough, but you get the idea. Something diplomatic. I figure it could stave them off for another couple of millennia.

PRESS SECRETARY: Oh, sure. You're not the one who has to go out there and float that kind of transparent crud at a press conference, are you?

CHIEF ADVISER: Well, there's no need to snap my head off, dear. What's the matter – your time of the month?

QUEEN (*aghast*): Oh my God, they don't know about *that* too, do they?

PROPAGANDA MINISTER: No, no, of course they don't know about *that*. My hunch is, they don't want to know anything at all about *that*.

PRESS SECRETARY: What I'm trying to say, Your Majesty, is that it's no picnic getting up in front of a roomful of male scribes to try to deny yesterday's denials, and buy them off with some limp little concession. It's not enough to admit to them they put us in the *mood*. These guys know we know more than we're letting on, and what they're asking among themselves now is, "What does the Queen know, in the biblical sense, and when did she know it?"

CHIEF ADVISER: Fine and dandy. It's no picnic right now, I agree with you. But what are the alternatives? Can you imagine what's going to ensue if you stand up in front of that pack of proud putative papas and start admitting they might have a real stake in parenthood? Next thing you know, Big Daddy'll be insisting the kid takes after *his* side of the family, and he'll want to turn him into a major-league pitcher instead of a respected surgeon.

PROPAGANDA MINISTER: The Chief Adviser's right, Your Majesty. The ramifications of this thing, if we don't manage to contain it, are too hideous even to contemplate. Once they find out they're the fathers of our country, next thing you know, they'll want to vote. After that, the clamour starts to own property, to get cast in major roles in family dramas, and to have their own statutory holiday, right after Mother's Day.

PRESS SECRETARY: You're telling me. Pretty soon they're buttoning their jackets the opposite way from ours, coaching midget hockey, and buying pipes.

QUEEN: Then there's no way back. Then we're into an era of men barbecuing out in the backyard in aprons with "What's Cookin', Good Lookin'?" on them. From that point, it's just a short step to defaulting on their child-support payments. Oh, ladies, is this what we want for the future of the world?

Of course, it wasn't what they wanted. But then, even as now, damage control is an imperfect art with limited effect. And so the rest, as they say, is history.

WORKING OUT

REWORKED

I know, I know. You don't have time for workout classes any more. Besides, you've heard all kinds of disturbing (yet spitefully satisfying) things about the deleterious effects of high-impact aerobics classes on the knees and feet. And anyway, there's a very nice Tai-Chi class being offered in a nearby church basement every second Wednesday, and you'll be getting to that just as soon as you find an evening clear. And, oh yes, if the Tai-Chi thing doesn't pan out, you've heard that swimming is the *only* total body exercise worth talking about, which means you'll be taking that up instead, the very minute they open up that new Y on the corner they're rumoured to be starting on any day now. In the meantime, though, you've been thinking very seriously that ballroom dancing (no, really) might be a fun way of getting into *some* kind of preliminary shape, and . . .

Hey, please. You don't have to make excuses to me. It's perfectly okay. And there's no need to feel guilty about the workout classes you're no longer taking either, because *I'm* taking your classes for you, along with my own, and I'm here to tell you that a lot about working out has been reworked since the last time you and I chatted about this subject.

For one thing, as you may already have heard, bouncing is out, and Low-Impact Aerobics and Stretch and Strength are in. This means that instead of exhausting yourself by jumping up and down, kicking from the knee, or jogging frantically on the spot to unlistenable music like some raw army recruit revving up to go over Disco Ridge, it is now possible for you to sweat and strain and suffer just as much by performing dull, unrewarding leg lifts, side stretches, and hip isolations that don't *look* like anything at all, but still manage to hurt like hell the next day.

There's even more good news. The clothes have changed again. You remember how the workout look went from jazz dance to high-rent wrestling, which meant that pretty pink tights and drooping leg-warmers gave way to striped jerseys, skintight Spandex overalls, and a dance belt? Well, *now* what's in is any bizarre mélange that strikes your fancy. EverLast tank-tops are big, especially when worn with torn tights and Reeboks.

You might also consider an oversized hand-painted and sequined sweatshirt (oh, this old thing) with ballooning nylon drawstring pants and Reeboks. Then there's jogging shorts worn over thick grey-wool tights and a shapeless holey T-shirt, which also make for a great look, when finished off by your Reeboks.

You'll notice there's a constant here. Reeboks comprise the one piece of brand-name gear that is *de rigueur* for the rigours of the workout-a-day world. Gone are the thirty-dollar Capezio flats of yore, or even the forty-buck high-heeled pumps you sported in your jazz-dance phase. Now it's sixty-dollar Reeboks or nothing, and not just any Reeboks will do. They must be lace-ups in white leather, freckled with myriad tiny perforations, looking for all the world like over-aged baby shoes.

Which may well be the key to their universal popularity. Working out is, as we know, distasteful, disheartening, and curiously lonely work, carried out in overheated, over-priced, and overcrowded studios traditionally located over stores with windows full of chic clothes that are still too skinny for you to get into, despite the fact that you've been working out four times a week for almost a year now, with other people's sweaty elbows flapping in your face and other people's white-leather Reeboks whacking up against the bridge of your nose as you lie on the floor performing pain-ful leg raises, going for the burn while you dream almost deliriously of going for the Aspirin.

Could it be, then, that those Reeboks serve as the one comforting clumsy and infantile element in a life otherwise too tense and mature? Would it be far-fetched to suggest that an overweight account executive in a torn T-shirt can happily regress in his Reeboks, as he lies kicking peevishly on the workout-studio floor, or that a sagging boutique manageress can gratefully relinquish all responsibility as she strains to touch her manicured fingers to her baby-bootied toes?

Or, if you find those possibilities untenable, consider this: Women's white-leather Reeboks look almost exactly like men's white-leather Reeboks, and thereunder, perhaps, lurks the subtext that explains what working out in the late 1980s is actually all about. It's no longer about allure and rampant sexuality, not in those trendily ravelled tights, stained misshapen old sweatshirts, and bumbly Reeboks. Not when the preferred musical accompaniment is disco-driven songs of hurt, betrayal, and deep mistrust, cranked up to an audial level that not only rebounds painfully against the eardrums, but also penetrates through every bodily pore and deep into the psyche, where the message that love hurts – even more than working out – can lodge and fester.

I'm not kidding. Because you haven't stared into the heart of darkness, quite frankly, until you've stood facing the mirror and the music in a crowded low-impact aerobics class, shoulder to shoulder with twenty other grim-faced strangers, repeatedly flexing your triceps in mindless unison, while from the stereo speakers a plaintive female voice protests, "Who's gonna be the next in line? Hope it's not a friend of mine . . . " as a way of reminding you that lovers are faithless and hope is in vain. Eventually you get to wondering, almost whimsically, why you're bothering to achieve physical perfection, when plainly there's nobody out there sincere enough to run the risk of attracting.

Perhaps it's all a subtle conditioning process devised by the scientific authorities to create and foster a new aversion to romance in a society suddenly swamped by the new moralism, and paralysed by the implications of AIDS. Maybe even the blundering genderlessness of those white Reeboks is part of the plan. And perhaps the final proof of this devilishly cleverly concocted pudding lies in the fact that workout classes are now routinely – and confidently – offered as early as nine o'clock on a Sunday morning.

You can easily tell who has spent Saturday night alone. These are the people who come bounding into the early-bird class, already attired in their workout togs, as indeed they have been since six-thirty or so, ready (nay, desperate) to burn off energy that, since the new celibacy, has absolutely no place else to go.

This is another reason, of course, that bitter ballads of betrayal provide absolutely essential accompaniment to the humiliation of flesh that is to follow. To toil through cold downtown streets on a dark winter Sunday morning, and arrive at an aerobics class to be met by the yearning strains of, say, "Unchained Melody", might be more than the human organism, however tautly tuned, could bear.

I don't know whether you've now reappraised your own defection from the workout regime in light of the new information that I've brought to you today. Have you begun to feel, in the last few minutes, that something vital is missing from your life, that could and should come thumping in on little Reebok-clad feet? Or has your mind started to stray, in an almost irresistible manner, back to thoughts of Tai-Chi and the new Y projected for construction on your corner round about 1996 or so? Or even to the creative possibilities inherent in sloth, overweight, and another helping of double-chocolate-and-orange-custard cake?

If so, believe me, no jury in the world would convict you, and neither would I. Although the Reeboks people will probably have a few sharp things to say.

A Canadian
Dramatic Classic

How often have you heard it said, in supermarket line-ups and gossipy barbershops, that the real problem with this country is that we have no long-standing dramatic tradition? It's an urgent concern that has long since superseded complaints about free trade and the way the butcher trimmed the meat, and no wonder. Apart from desultory efforts in earlier centuries, the criticism runs, the history of original Canadian drama is so short as to be virtually negligible. And a country without a long theatrical tradition, the critics continue, is a country whose drama by necessity will be tentative, rootless, and devoid of real distinction.

Whether this argument is absolutely true or not, it's pervasive enough to have worked its debilitating influence on the Canadian consciousness, with the result that the country is full of people who experience feelings of anxiety and inferiority whenever the words "native theatre" are mentioned. Which is why I've taken it upon myself to soothe the national psyche by devising, albeit belatedly, a play that will instantly become a classic and reign for all time as THE PROGENITOR OF MODERN CANADIAN DRAMA.

No small task, of course, and some nit-pickers might object that one play, however breathtaking in scope and comprehensive in theme, is simply not sufficient, in and of itself, to constitute an entire tradition. To those people I can only say, let's see you do better in the time available. At least when I sat down to write the definitive Canadian classic, I exerted every effort to make it a real humdinger.

American family-oriented drama and the tradition of European "kitchen sink" naturalism are, we know, very strong in contemporary Canadian theatre, which is why I thought it would be appropriate to choose inspiration from seminal works in this field. The result – *Long Days Awake With My Single Sister Irene* – will, I trust, meet with enthusiastic acclaim, and merit the thanks of the Canadian theatre community, grateful that, at last, Canada has an illustrious artistic past to which we can point with pride, and reminisce about at the expense of the present.

LONG DAYS AWAKE WITH MY SINGLE SISTER IRENE

A classic in three acts – I know, I know, most classics are in four or five acts, but this, remember, is a Canadian classic. Frankly, even three acts seems pushy.

The Characters
RHONDA ⎫
MONA   ⎬ Three sisters
IRENE ⎭
PAPA – the patriarch, and also Prime Minister of Canada
MAMA – once devout and girlish, now ravaged by the effects
    of prolonged addiction to American pop culture
JAMIE – the elder son, a dissolute Broadway sport and Canadian film producer

MAURIE – the younger brother, torn between his dual loves, the violin and the hockey stick

The ZEYDA – the grandfather, philosophical about being the only Jew in the family

The action of the play takes place in the family home, above a Canadian Tire store in a large urban centre in Canada.

Act One

(*The lights come up in the living-room, where* RHONDA, *a teacher of English as a Second Language, is correcting assignments at a table.* MONA, *her married sister, whistles "Here Comes the Bride" without much tune but lots of irony, and* IRENE, *the youngest, an aspiring actress, thumbs through the Actors' Equity newsletter on the settee.*)

RHONDA: Just think – on this very day, the fifth of May, a year ago, Papa died. On your birthday, Irene. Today, exactly one year later, is the fifth of May as well, *and* your birthday, which seems extraordinary to me. It was very cold then, as now; snow was falling.

MONA (*drily*): Naturally.

RHONDA: Now a year has passed, and snow is still falling. The very same snow, I shouldn't be surprised. A year has passed, my dear sisters, and we can think of Papa's death quite calmly. Who would ever have believed, a year ago, that might be so?

MONA (*ironically*): It is so, my dear Rhonda, because Papa did not, in fact, die. He merely threatened to, as he so often does, and, once more, it turned out to be an idle promise. Just once, I wish our papa would carry out one single thing he vows to do.

RHONDA: Don't whistle, Mona. It makes my head ache so dreadfully.

MONA (*drolly*): I wasn't whistling. I was speaking. *This*, my dear sister, is whistling. (*She resumes whistling "Here Comes the Bride".*)

IRENE (*looking up from the Equity newsletter*): I don't know why I'm so happy today. There certainly are not any auditions worth talking about in here. And yet I woke up this morning, remembered that it was my birthday, and all at once I felt so joyful. I thought back to my childhood, when there were so many roles for talented juveniles. Not like now, when actresses are a kopek a dozen and decent parts as rare as Teflon samovars.

MONA (*tensely*): Yes, what a wretched city this is, to be sure. Nothing but touring shows and bad stock productions out of New York. My poor Irene and her blighted career! If only we were in Moose Jaw, things would be so different.

RHONDA (*puts down her marking-pen*): Yes, dear, dear Moose Jaw! To go back to Moose Jaw, and quickly!

PAPA (*entering*): Here, what's all this? Jawing on about Moose Jaw again? And what's wrong with here, I'd like to know? By Jove, I've made a fine home for you here, in the city, even if that snivelling coward of a brother of yours happens not to think so.

RHONDA: There, there. Nothing is wrong with Maurie, Papa. Only that he sits all the day in his room, trying to decide whether to practise the violin or to tape his hockey stick.

PAPA: I meant your other brother, Jamie, that no-good ingrate, always filling your heads with lying poison about going back to Moose Jaw.

IRENE (*runs to her father, throws her arms about his neck*): Dear Papa, when I woke up this morning, suddenly it all came clear to me!

PAPA: Your birthday, I know. That's right, throw it in my face. The way you throw everything, like what's happened to your mother.

IRENE: No, no! I did not for a minute expect a present. I know how generosity was ground out of your nature long years ago, Papa. We've heard the story of your early days as an Irish urchin in this country many, many times.

PAPA: Keep your scornful tongue off my origins. They're what got me elected, and have kept me elected, seven consecutive terms. But it's a curse, too. I've always said it, anything that comes too easily and goes on too long, even a cushy job, is a curse. By heaven, girls, if we lived in the States, like a respectable family, they'd have tossed me out of office after two terms, and your mother might never have become a – what she is.

MONA (*sourly*): Nevertheless, Papa, Irene has her little speech about the dignity of work to make, and you must let her. It is her birthday, you know.

PAPA: Yes, Irene loves to make speeches. The only one of this accursed tribe that takes after the old man.

MONA (*sullenly*): It is not easy for us, Papa. We are not Irish.

IRENE: Dear Papa, I've thought about it, and I know all about it now. A man must work by the sweat of his brow – unless, of course, he is in politics, like you. All the purpose and meaning of life is bound up in work. How invigorating, for instance, to get up at dawn and break stones by the road-side, or to be a schoolteacher. Like you, Rhonda – trying to din irregular verbs into the heads of new Canadians who will only end up relegated to menial jobs where grammar does not matter!

RHONDA: Yes, I know. Why do you suppose, my dear little sister, that my head aches so?

IRENE: I'd rather be a shepherd or even an ox than an out-of-work actress, calling her agent four times a day and turning up for commercial auditions in the wrong clothes!

JAMIE (*sauntering in*): Too true, little lady, and don't I know it. But let me tell you, none of this would be happening if you'd bankroll my notion of a little film-production facility back in Moose Jaw.

PAPA: I might have known! Filling your sisters' heads with your sick poison, and on Irene's birthday, too, for shame.

JAMIE: It's time someone told the truth here, Papa, and you've been lying too long at constituency meetings to volunteer for the job. This family has no business living over a Canadian Tire store in a big, faceless city. Regionalism is what's made Canada great, and Moose Jaw could be a centre for films of integrity, if you'd listen to me. But you won't listen, not even on my sister's birthday, and if she lives to see another one, I'd be damned surprised. What with this summer cold of hers.

IRENE: I have the same cold as everyone else, truly. It's a winter cold, that carries on the year round. Is that not so?

RHONDA: There, there, my dear sister, calm yourself.

MAMA (*entering, her hair streaming*): What is all this talk about colds? I won't have it, Papa, I simply won't.

PAPA: No one here has a cold, Mama. Especially not Irene.

MAMA (*too bright*): Because, you know, if she has a cold, it's the simplest thing to get rid of. I was just reading about it, in this week's *People*. When Morgan Fairchild has a cold, she takes a cup of boiling water, ginger-root, and some Vitamin C! (*Pause, then nervously, pats her hair.*) Why . . . why is everyone looking at me? Is something wrong with my hair?

JAMIE (*bitterly*): Oh, Mama, how could you?

MONA (*acerbicly, to* JAMIE): How could *you*? "Bitterly" is *my* stage direction. My very own.

PAPA: Mama, what's to become of you? You promised, on your word of honour!

MAMA: Why, Papa, I have no idea what you mean.

JAMIE: He means you promised to quit, Mama, but now you're back on the junk.

MAMA: Jamie! What a way to speak to your mother!

JAMIE: I know the game. *People* magazine, *Rambo* retrospectives, *Wheel of Fortune, The Beach Boys' Greatest Hits*. You promised to kick the habit, but now you're hooked again, aren't you, Mama? Admit it! You're nothing but a lying Yankee pop-culture hophead!

MAMA: Don't scold, Jamie. Papa, don't look at me like that. Girls, this is none of your business, you're not even from the same play. It's those sleepless nights in the spare room, listening to the snow ploughs. . . . And the snow! The awful, muffling snow. I could be strong and stand up to anything, if it weren't for the snow and the mournful cry of those snow ploughs!

MAURIE (*appearing from his bedroom*): Say, Mama, I'll tell you what. What say we pack up the whole fam-damily and head back to Moose Jaw? Sure! No snow there, I bet. Whaddaya say, Jamie?

RHONDA (*goes to him*): Maurie, my dearest little brother! But tell me, are you not meant to be in your room, practising your violin and taping your hockey stick?

MAURIE: With all this noise, who can concentrate? Say, I got confused, started practising my hockey stick and taping the violin. Besides, I got to wondering. What's become of the Zeyda? He's taken a powder, although none of the Canadian Tire money, you should excuse the expression, took a hike with him.

MONA (*softly*) Tararaboomdeeyay . . .

RHONDA: Oh truly, Mona, you're not helping.

MAURIE: Last I remember, the Zeyda was slurping tea out of a glass and reading Marx in the kitchen, and complaining as usual about being the only Jewish person in the family. Although, what can I say? I try.

JAMIE: God, I wish the Zeyda would get off that damned morbid kick of his. Look at the girls here, they never complain. Even though they have to do all their lines in translation, and it's a pretty damned stilted translation at that.

PAPA (*to JAMIE*): Now, if that's not you all over, looking down your nose at everything, including the translation. A lot you care, my boyo, that the Zeyda's gone missing, most likely on the roof again, reading his godless Karl Marx, instead of the works of a good Irish Catholic like John Diefenbaker.

MAMA (*detached*): I think I'd like to lie down in the spare room and take a nap. . . .

JAMIE (*to MONA*): Uh-oh. You know what that means. More American magazines and TV shows, and blockbuster Alternate Selections from the Book-of-the-Month Club. (*To MAURIE*) And as for you, kid . . . you keep on playing shinny with those kids down on the corner, it's curtains for a career with the fiddle.

MAURIE: Say, how do you figure that? What, you think I shoot a puck with my *hands*?

JAMIE: I'm telling you, it's curtains, and it's never been anything but, for this whole accursed family!

(*Whether or not* JAMIE's *right is up for debate, but at this point it's certainly curtains for Act One of* Long Days

Awake With My Single Sister Irene. *When the curtain rises on Act Two, we discover that the* ZEYDA *is indeed up on the roof, threatening to jump unless another Jewish (or at the very least a left-leaning) character is written into the script.*

PAPA goes up onto the roof to reason with him, and to point out that the three sisters are Russian, which is practically the same thing as Marxist, even if they do date from Czarist Russia. But the ZEYDA *is unimpressed, and* PAPA *returns from the roof angry and defeated, to join the rest of the family in the drawing-room, under the mistaken impression that an art class must be in progress.*

The only family members clearly uninterested in discussing the Zeyda problem are MAMA, *surreptitiously perusing vacation brochures in the spare room while the snow ploughs continue their mournful chorus, and* MONA, *too preoccupied with her personal life to spare a thought for anyone else.*

Although married, MONA *has for some time been carrying on a passionate affair with a Mountie of Ukrainian-Canadian descent named* VERSHENKO, *whose detachment is housed in a nearby barracks. The pathos of the situation is accentuated by the fact that* VERSHENKO *is also married, to a hypochondriacal woman continually in a fit of pique because she is never seen onstage.* MONA *chats with him in a corner of the drawing-room in low tones, so as not to be overheard by the other characters, yet somehow contrives to be perfectly audible to the four hundred complete strangers in the audience.)*

MONA (*with quiet irony*): Yes, of course, I quite understand the situation with your wife. My husband, for instance, continually whines at me, "It's not my fault; it's not my fault; I am only an offstage character." As though there were something *I* could do about it!

PAPA (*loudly*): Damn it, what kind of drawing-room is this, I'd like to know? Without a stick of charcoal or so much as a sheet of sketch paper to bless itself with!

MONA (*bitterly*): On the other hand, there are also some onstage characters whose flaws are no less unappealing.

VERSHENKO: I love you, dear lady, love, love . . .

MONA (*tensely*): Hush! You must not say such things to me.

VERSHENKO: Then to whom? To my horse, Bobik, shifting from one foot to the other in the stable, dreaming of the day when he and I will be promoted from the postcards to performing together in the Musical Ride?

MONA (*rigidly*): True. As Gogol says, "Friends, if you must be a horse, at least be a star." Oh, if only we were back in Moose Jaw!

JAMIE: For God's sake, Papa, what I told you before, about a drawing-room being a room to draw in, that was only the bunk. Strictly to keep your mind off Mama, and off government policy, too.

RHONDA: Jamie's right, Papa, for once in a way. There's nothing, nothing, we can do for poor dear Mama, locked up in the spare room, investigating hotel rates at the Epcot Center. As for your poor, hopeless policies –

PAPA: What's wrong with conscription, I'd like to know? I ran on it in three successful campaigns.

RHONDA: But there is no war on now, Papa. Oh, how my head aches. I shall give up pointillism straightaway! (*Lays down her paint-brush.*)

VERSHENKO (*to MONA*): In two or three hundred years, of course, Moose Jaw won't seem so important. The first time I mixed in bran with Bobik's oats, for instance, he was beside himself with delight. But after three or four times, he took the bran for granted, with a grain of salt, you might almost say. Just in that manner, soon you will tire of Moose Jaw and its thousand delights. Do you take my meaning, dear lady? We have no happiness. We only wish we did, and sigh accordingly.

MONA (*warily*): How can you be so sure of these things?

VERSHENKO: Dear lady, I am *from* Moose Jaw, and could not wait to leave.

MAURIE: Say, Papa, all the time I'm in my room, taping up that stick and practising my scales, my brain is humming

like the Algoma and Northern on a fast track in the rain!
"Clackety-clack, hockey or fiddle, hockey or fiddle?" Call
me bughouse, Papa, but that's the refrain.

PAPA: Just don't make my mistake, boyo, and get trapped in
a job because it's easy and you're good at it.

JAMIE: That's not how the parliamentary press gallery tells
it.

PAPA: Can you not shut your indolent Broadway mouth one
minute, or else make yourself useful for once, you laya-
bout loafer, by going up to the roof to talk a scrap of sense
into the Zeyda? Which is about all you can spare, you dissolute faker, one scrap of sense.

VERSHENKO (*rises*): Dear lady, I must be off. It's my wife.

MONA (*vaguely*): But . . . how do you know?

VERSHENKO: One learns to sense these things. She is up on
the roof again, threatening to jump.

MONA (*tearfully*): Truly, I know the feeling.

VERSHENKO: Now, now. Moose Jaw does not believe in tears.
(*Kisses her hand.*) Farewell. (*He exits.*)

MONA (*angrily, to the others*): That's right! Quarrel about your
art supplies! Take up the evening with reproaches about
Mama! Bide your time until our skinflint Papa finally
breaks out his bargain-basement whiskey!

IRENE: Mona, how can you!

MONA (*raggedly*): And you, Irene? Who has more right to be
cross than you? An entire act, and not one single line to
call your own! How has this happened?

(*At this point, the other characters all look at each other
in confusion as the curtain falls, for in fact no one else
has noticed that* IRENE *has had nothing to say since Act
One.* JAMIE *departs to the roof, which means, perhaps,
that help is on the way for the* ZEYDA.

PAPA *worries that news of* MAMA'S *new re-addiction to
American culture will get out to the press, to compromise
his free-trade initiatives with the United States. And*
MONA *is left alone to ponder why her little brother* MAURIE
finds it necessary to start every sentence with "Say!")

However, when the curtain rises on Act Three, we feel ourselves no closer to answers to those haunting questions, although at least the snow ploughs have, for the moment, ceased their prehistoric wails. Much else has changed in the family's situation as well. The Mountie detachment has, without warning, been reassigned – under a new regional-equity program initiated by PAPA's *government – to, of all places, Moose Jaw.*

MONA, *therefore, has been forced not only to say farewell forever to Corporal* VERSHENKO, *her red-coated love, but to face up to the fact that she has simultaneously run out of bracketed adverbs to accompany her pithy utterances.* VERSHENKO *swears he will love her forever, and phone at those times when rate reductions apply, but in her heart,* MONA *knows it is over between them.*

JAMIE *is still up on the roof reasoning with the* ZEYDA, *although his physical absence from the scene has not prevented him from arranging a film deal that includes members of the family. Production has begun on this project, a new Canadian feature film, with* MAURIE *as a tortured young man torn between his twin devotions to the accordion and the lacrosse stick.* IRENE *also has a part, as the Special Business Extra in one of the lacrosse tournament scenes who gets knocked unconscious when a lacrosse ball comes screaming into the crowd. All other significant roles in the film are played by Americans.*

As day darkens into night, the family gathers around the kitchen table and sinks deeper and deeper into contemplation of the past. All except PAPA, *who sinks deeper and deeper into successive glasses of cheap bar-brand whiskey, as he frets about the fact that* JAMIE *has gone into the film business only to spite him, and worries that news of* MONA's *truncated affair with the Mountie Corporal* VERSHENKO *will hit the papers just in time for the upcoming election.*

Still, he resolves to make one last attempt to communicate with the tattered remnants of what was once his family.)

PAPA: Sure, and don't think I don't know what you all think of the old man –

MONA (*adverblessly*): Tararaboomdeeyay.

RHONDA: Don't whistle, Mona. My head aches so.

PAPA (*drunk, Irish, and oblivious*): But it's the past that does things to us we cannot help, nor cannot change.

MONA: As the poet says, "Who would eat winnebagos, when potatoes are so cheap?"

IRENE: I must never say this to Jamie, but the work on the film is so tedious and exhausting that I feel certain sometimes that I will lose my mind. (*Tearfully*) In fact, it's almost a certainty that I am losing my mind. Just yesterday, I tried to remember the difference between "downstage" and "upstage" and I could not! Nor could I recall, for the life of me, the word for that part off to the side where you stand waiting for your cue to come on! The "wings", of course, the "wings"! But do you think I could come up with the word on my own? Oh, my dear sisters, I trained for so many years to be a stage actress, and now look how it has all turned out! I spend my days taking and retaking the scene in the film where I get slammed in the mouth by a lacrosse ball. And you, Rhonda, think *you* have a headache? (*To* MAURIE) And you, little brother. You do nothing now but play that accursed violin.

MAURIE: Say, it beats the accordion. You know what, late at night, I get the yen sometimes – and I don't mean a Chinee coin – to get up and go beyond where the snow ploughs are droning. Any place where things are happening and the prospect of a meaningful social revolution still exists.

PAPA: Fine talk! Is this why I crossed the sea to this country, and blackened boots in a sweatshop for twenty cents a week, then got control of my party and turned myself into the longest-serving Prime Minister this land has ever known? So that my own son could blather that species of Marxist gabble that accomplishes nothing apart from creating embarrassing headlines for the old man?

(*Suddenly* JAMIE *enters triumphantly with the* ZEYDA *in tow.*)

JAMIE: Look what I found up on the roof.

THE OTHERS: Zeyda! How are you? Etc., etc.

ZEYDA: Nu? A man is not a piece fruit. (*Shrugs*.) On the other hand, a man is not a pigeon either, which is what you'd have to be to stand what's up on that roof. Feh! Such filth. Nu, who's got a glass tea for the Zeyda?

PAPA: Here, Zeyda, have a glass whiskey – er, a glass of whiskey – instead. (*Sotto voce to* JAMIE) How'd you lure him down, lad?

JAMIE (*uncomfortably*): What does it matter how, Papa? He's down, isn't he? Just give me a little credit for something for once.

ZEYDA: And so tell me, where do I sign, for this once-in-a-lifetime movie deal? If I'm selling out the workers and the revolution already, I might as well get on with it.

MAURIE (*to* JAMIE): Selling out! Say, what does he mean, big brother?

JAMIE (*snarls*): Yeah, I suppose you're mistrustful as hell of me, thinking back to what I said before, about doing anything for a buck. Well, it's true. You're all damn fine folks, but I'm a rotten, twisted no-good, who's sold the family down the river, just for spite. You might as well hear the straight dope – I've sold my film company – to the Americans. Maurie and Irene are out of work, as of now. But the Zeyda's been signed to a three-picture deal, commencing with a screwball shtetl comedy called *Kiss My Mezuzah* with Chevy Chase to co-star and the Police Academy gang to produce and direct.

MONA: You say you've sold the production company? To strangers? And with it, all hope for returning home to Moose Jaw?

PAPA: I hate like poison to say it of my first-born, but you're an ingrate swine who's to blame for every single thing wrong in this family, including what's happened to Mama.
(*In the background, we hear hammering sounds as the Americans begin construction of a sound stage. And then, even louder, the discordant crash of accordion notes.*)

MAURIE: Say, it didn't take those Americans long to find some other chump for my accordion scenes. I – say, isn't this Mama?

(Indeed it is. MAMA *enters, hair in wild disarray, playing the accordion with one hand, and, in the other, tenderly carrying a battered old Canadian Tire catalogue. She is lost in the past.)*

MAMA: Has anyone seen the Canadian Tire money? There are so many things I want to buy from the catalogue. I don't know why I ever abandoned Canadian Tire, and became hooked on Neiman-Marcus and Baskin-Robbins and Bonwit-Teller in the first place. I didn't set out to be an American pop-culture junkie, I know that. But something happened to me . . . What was it? Ah, I remember now. It was in the spring of my senior year – although we Canadians do not call it "senior year". I spent a weekend in Minot, North Dakota, and fell in love with J. C. Penney, and was so happy for a time.

RHONDA: Oh, my dear sisters, listen to the sound of the hammers as the Americans build and build! Our life is not ended yet. In just a little while, we shall know how we got into this play with these people, and who's to blame. It seems as though a little more, and we shall know what kind of copyright laws cover a situation like this, and why we live and why we suffer over a Canadian Tire store with a pack of strangers.

IRENE: It's the Zeyda who worries me. Who on earth he is, and how he can drink tea from a glass, when he doesn't even appear to be Russian?

MONA: If only we knew. If only we knew.

(The curtain falls.)

Great Dames

The maître d' is the first person to approach us in the Italian restaurant. "Yes, dear, can I help you?"

Dear. My friend and I exchange a look. The maître d' is all of twenty-three years old. Whereas my friend and I are a month or so older than that.

Once we're seated, the busboy shows up with a basket of rolls. "Bread, ma'am?" Another look passes between us, as we instantly shrivel into grannies licensed to tote a cane.

By the time the waiter comes to take our order, we are braced for the worst. Sure enough, right on schedule, the worst arrives. "Something from the bar for you ladies tonight?"

Ladies! Dear and ma'am are bad enough, but I will *not* be a lady. Whatever happened to the good old days, and those

non-squirm-making terms of female endearment? Like –
well, like "dame".

I would have been honoured to be a dame. A dame was
the brisk and plucky sort of woman epitomized by Norma
Shearer or Mary Astor, with a crisp perm, pearls, and elbow-
length gloves. While my friend and I schlep into Italian restaurants porting flopping hi-tech tote bags made from an old
bus tire, a dame would have sashayed in on spectator
pumps, carrying a smart little clutch.

Dames had Sealyham terriers on little braided leashes,
instead of a slobbery mutt named Ephraim we modern
ladies succumbed to in a moment of weakness at the Animal
Shelter. Dames got to wear hats, managed not to look cheap
in leopard-patterned pyjamas, drove something called a
roadster, and – best of all – lived in an age when smoking
cigarettes didn't hurt you one bit.

What exactly was it that made things so different then?
After thinking it over carefully, I've decided it was all in the
phraseology. Back in those days, a dame could be frequently
heard to exclaim, "Say! Isn't this simply grand?" Grand.
Instead of relevant, evocative, significant, or resonant,
which is about as good as things ever get in our convoluted
times.

Okay, so the men dames were forced to associate with
were often along the undernourished lines of William Powell
and Fred Astaire. Men given to a trifle too much lip-rouge
and a tad too little hair. So what?

Let me tell you something, at least those guys turned *up*
– and in heartening abundance. And they were never afraid
to commit, not even from the first moment. "Say," they'd
say to the dame, "you're quite a dame, sister. Isn't this
grand?" And bingo, they'd be off to the races in the roadster.

Now, maybe the life of a dame doesn't appeal to you. In
that case, you might have preferred being a gal. Galhood was
in flower during the Second World War, and with very little
effort on her part, any enterprising sister could make herself
look like Ann Sheridan or Katharine Hepburn.

Gals were sportier than dames. They wore tweed jackets
and pageboy bobs, and wedgies, and had jettisoned the Sea-

lyham in favour of a set of golf clubs. Instead of "Say!" a
gal exclaimed, "Good golly!" Otherwise, it was pretty much
the same as damehood. You know – grand?

Chances are, your mother or your grandmother was a
dame or a gal, or a bit of both. My mother spent her twenties
and thirties in a now-extinct article of clothing called a
"housedress", and went out in hats with little half-veils and
earrings that screwed on. And when my mother went down
the concrete front walk, her open-toed pumps made a brisk
sound exactly like "Kiss-kass-korss".

I suppose at some level we ladies of the eighties still look
back at the dames and gals who were our mothers and
grandmothers as the *real* women, and envy them a species
of feminine certainty that we seem to lack.

Although, on second thought, maybe things weren't quite
as idyllic as all that. I still remember how utterly uncom-
prehending I was as a small child when my mother
announced her sudden intention to take swimming lessons.
And how mortified I was when she was subsequently the
only mother to show up at my ballet class with wet wiggly
hair.

Even worse, there was the infamous day that, just for fun,
she leapt onto my brother's bicycle and pedalled all around
the neighbourhood, housedress flapping in the wind. There
was an infestation of giant brown dragonflies that summer,
and it was hard to tell which was the more appalling sight
out the front window – the sky full of dragonflies swooping
and performing double Immelmanns, or the spectacle of my
mother on a bike. Grown-up women over thirty, I recall telling her sternly, didn't do things like that. It is a tribute to
my mother's good-sport galhood that, thirty years later, she
watches without comment as I mount my own bike.

"Here are your drinks, ladies," says the waiter, and my
friend and I exchange another grimace, before proposing a
toast. To the dames and gals who left us everything we have
today – except a name we can stand being called. Say,
though, weren't they simply grand?

AUTO-NOMY

I can't explain how I determined that the right moment had come to get a car of my own. Lord knows, when I made the announcement, it stunned practically everyone. Not only am I famous among my friends as a fiercely militant cyclist (Bikes Don't Kill, Cars Do), I am equally renowned as one of the great *schnorrers* of our time when it comes to cadging rides.

You motorists are familiar with my type, I'm sure. It's about 2 a.m. at a party and – since it's a weekend night in October – a blizzard is raging outside. You have already braved the storm once to scrape your windshield with a bare and stiffened hand, and then a second time to help dig out the hapless jerk who's blocking your way out of the drive.

You duck back into the house one more time to empty the snow out of your socks and to thank your host for luring you out of your own warm den to enjoy tepid food, tepid drinks, and even tepider company before turning your face back into the storm for the long, cold ride home. And guess who's hovering in the doorway, coat all buttoned up and a smile of sickly ingratiation on her face?

Me, that's who. Hoping to be dropped up in the 'burbs, although your destination is the southernmost edge of town.

To motorists, therefore, it will come as a relief to learn of my decision to buy a car, and don't think I don't know the revenge you're plotting on me. How many of you will call to ask me if I could swing by Detroit to pick you up on my way to the park. Or will appear miraculously at the opera with no way home and incipient pleurosis on the rainiest night of the year. Or will force me to work out empirically exactly how many feet of your old barn siding can be forced into my hatchback.

But it serves me right, and I am willing to embrace all aspects of car ownership, even the Hammurabi-esque revenge my motoring friends will exact. Because there is still absolutely nothing in North American society that proclaims adult status so precisely as owning a car.

Getting a dog comes close, since a dog requires approximately the same level of care and attention. Although it can be argued that I don't really *need* to go out to the driveway to visit the car quite as often as I do, since my sense that the poor thing looks lonely sitting out there may well be a trick of the light on the windshield.

Buying a house or having a child (known as the Big Ones in the circles I move in) are too extreme as far as mere declarations of maturity go. One ought not carry the notion of adulthood quite *that* far, not unless there are other, purer motives involved. Car ownership, on the other hand, need proceed from no loftier a goal than to finally make yourself feel like the grown-up you've been looking like for so many years now. And even if that's all you're in it for, it's perfectly okay.

Somehow, opening the door of your very own car, climbing

in, throwing a briefcase full of work into the back seat, and purring off to the office make you more of a businesslike person in your own eyes than piling that same work into your backpack and unchaining the bike. And if you can find a parking lot to overcharge you into the bargain, then your sense of sophisticated maturity is that much more enhanced.

Perhaps because first-car ownership has come to me relatively late in life, I may seem to be making too much of all this. But after years of mooching rides, nervously borrowing the cars of friends, and renting what seems like the same red Chevette again and again to revel in the sensation of going from zero to twelve miles an hour in eighteen seconds flat, I have learned one thing for sure: the illusion of maturity cannot be achieved by driving any car other than your very own.

I can recall the day when I was sixteen, newly licensed and all dressed up to take myself for a spin in my mother's aged Morris. I had my hair swept up in the Grecian curls so fashionable in those days (a period in history roughly concurrent with the Peloponnesian Wars), as much blue eyeliner as the law would allow, a new coat, and a brand-new chiffon scarf that exactly matched my cotton gloves. It's the same look I'm going to try for at the ceremony when they award me the Nobel Prize.

As I tooled along – and in a Morris, you could *tool* – I lit up a cigarette to complete the picture of absolute adulthood. No sooner was the cigarette lodged between my lips than I passed some people I knew. Delighted at the opportunity to call attention to the poised picture I made behind the wheel, I tooted the horn and mouthed, "Hi!" as I rolled by. Unfortunately, in opening my mouth to form that single syllable, I caused the cigarette to fall – straight into the folds of my new chiffon scarf.

Chiffon burns just as eagerly as you might think, and by the time I managed to pull the car over, smoke was pouring from my chest. The friends I'd rolled so regally past came running, to find me shrieking and shaking the scarf (now marred by a hundred burn holes) as I tried to locate the smouldering cigarette buried within.

To this day, I am convinced that if it had been *my* car rather than my mother's, such a thing would never have happened to undermine my elegant image. But, just as a precaution, now that I have a car of my own, I intend never ever to wear chiffon behind the wheel again.

A lot else has changed in my life, too, since my car came into the picture. Her name is Emily Car (Deborah Car was rejected as insufficiently nationalistic) and I find myself reacting to the responsibilities of ownership with all the guilt-ridden sensitivity appropriate to my age, sex, and psychic make-up. But even *I* didn't realize the degree to which my protective instincts had gotten out of hand until a puzzling document turned up in Emily's glove compartment, secreted away underneath the Owner's Manual.

At first I could make no sense of the rather clumsy scrawl, but gradually, by dint of much frowning scrutiny, a pattern in the script began to emerge, and I finally understood what I had on my hands: Emily Car has been keeping a diary.

Day One. "Dear Diary. Well, it's happened at last. Someone has bought me. I can't say how I feel about her yet. She came onto the lot with a copy of *Lemon-Aid* tucked under her arm, and a glint of consumerist suspicion in her eye, and the first thing I overheard her tell the salesman was that she *had* to have a convertible coupe in two harmonizing shades of pink. Since I am a four-door hardtop in a solid blue, I naturally took for granted that that was the end of that.

"But the next thing you know, the salesman was giving her the familiar line about how the stock is low at the end of the model year, and how badly the convertibles leak. (When the convertibles are overstocked, of course he talks about how stuffy the hardtops are in summer.) Then he brought her over to look at me.

"When I saw the suspicious glaze in her eye melt, and a soppy maternal expression pass over her face, I knew she was a goner. I *am* definitely the cutest thing on the lot. Why, just last week that pickup truck tried to pick me up."

Day Two. "Dear Diary, it seems like only yesterday that my new owner drove me off the lot, but already I'm beginning to have serious qualms about the shape my new life is taking. For starters, she's given me a name and, frankly, I find that sort of thing a bit icky and weird. Then there's the fact that she's hardly taken me out of the garage. Yesterday she planned to drive some place, but changed her mind when it clouded up and took the bus instead.

"Today, when she did take me out, a chestnut fell on my hood at a stoplight, and she started to cry and immediately headed for home. Thank God I started this diary; otherwise I'd go crazy from the boredom."

Day Three. "A secondary problem has surfaced in my new existence. Her bicycle, with whom I'm forced to share the garage, is becoming a real pain in the crankcase. First of all, the damn thing is jealous, although I'm hard put to figure out *why*. Not only does it get taken out a lot more often than I do – especially in the rain – but yesterday our owner bought it a new bell so that it won't feel supplanted by me. Fat chance.

"So I have the bike's hostile rivalry to contend with, and in addition, like all two-wheelers, it's a real ecological snob. It's constantly making snide references to emission control and noise pollution, to which I try to pay no attention. Happily, I've struck up quite a congenial acquaintance with the power mower, which naturally annoys the heck out of the bike, ha ha."

Day Four. "It turns out that one of the reasons I never get to go any place is that she doesn't know how to find the entrance ramp onto the parkway. It never ceases to amaze me how sheltered these downtown-dwelling erstwhile pedestrians are. Do you know, she had to have someone show her how to fill gas at a self-serve, she hasn't a clue where the big food terminals are, and she's never once listened to a traffic report while stalled in a jam at rush-hour?"

Day Five. "Dear Diary. Today was possibly the most traumatic to date. Not for me – for her. First, she took me to the car-wash. (There was apparently a millimetre of bird-dropping on my roof.) Watching me being pulled through the spraying hoses and huge buffeting brushes was too much for her. She started to cry.

"Then it was off to the automotive shop to install a radio

and a tape deck. Not for *her*, of course. She doesn't drive me often enough to require entertainment. No, the radio's for *me*, she says. To keep me and the power mower company in the garage while she's out in the rain on the bike.

"She cried at the automotive shop, too. Not only did she hate to leave me there for the installation, but she made a complete spectacle of herself in front of the serviceman before she left. She demanded to know exactly what was involved in putting in a radio, and whether or not it was going to hurt me. If only I could tell her that what *really* hurts me is being smothered with this kind of attention.

"But you know, Dear Diary, there's another aspect to all of this, even more upsetting than going through these experiences and then having to recount them for posterity. As I was saying to the power mower just the other day, what really gives me the gears is knowing that whoever, in succeeding generations, finds my diary and reads what I've written here will never, for even a single second, believe one word of it."

Hot-Blooded
Latin Lovers

The kind of person who enjoyed Latin as a kid grows up into a certain kind of adult – an adult possessed of a sense of fraternity with all the other grown-up kids who enjoyed Latin too, once upon a time.

It's hard to pinpoint the personality type of the hot-blooded Latin fan. Can it be identified by a sense of awestruck appreciation for the breathless finality of the Ablative Absolute? Or a deep-seated yearning for the orderly no-nonsense goals exemplified by the Dative of Purpose?

Loving Latin, of course, goes far beyond a flair for declension or an overwhelming desire to memorize the conjugation of the Future Imperfect of the verb "impero, imperare". Those who love Latin also revel in the stiff syntactical formalities of some of its unlikelier constructions: "Caesar believed his legions to be advancing with the greatest possible haste." "Be unwilling, O Pompey, to profess yourself an enemy of the state."

The best part about Latin, of course, is the fact that you can't do one useful thing with it later on. Phrases like the preceding won't get the salt passed, or your pants pressed, or impress a waiter in a Roman restaurant, or get you stamps sufficient to send a postcard airmail overseas.

The only useful thing about Latin, in fact, was that back in high school, when such considerations were crucial, Latin served to get you out of a whole bunch of other things you didn't want to do. Kids who took Latin got to drop Physics or Typing class. Latin was perfect for those who hated Home Ec, or felt themselves unwilling, O Pompey, to learn to construct a magazine rack in Woodworking class.

Not that Latinophiles were brilliant scholars in any other respect. We couldn't converse in living languages worth a damn, or untangle the mysteries of the logarithmic table, or commit historical dates to memory along with our irregular Latin verbs, or figure out how it was that it took two hydrogens to accomplish the task of mating with a single morsel of oxygen.

All we could do with any degree of aptitude was to burrow down into an unsavoury heap of participles and gerunds and fourth-declension nouns in the vocative case, and verbs in the past pluperfect, and then emerge minutes later, flushed and triumphant, brandishing a more or less accurately translated page of Cicero. It was a kind of party trick, like being able to read billboards backward, or separate the rings of a Chinese puzzle, or memorize the serial numbers on dozens of boxcars rolling by.

We were the kind of people who could look at a word like "villatic" and immediately figure out what it might mean, solely according to its Latin root. We had no trouble using "compluvium" in a sentence, and if an aphorism was ever required in a tense situation, we were always the ones who could be counted upon to quip, "Per ardua ad astra," when the moment was right.

Latin teachers were, of course, warped adult versions of our own quirky and anomalous selves – with skin conditions, or thick Scottish accents, or a predilection for nibbling the chalk. At the school I went to, teaching Latin to the few girls socially maladjusted enough to continue taking it year after year always devolved upon the most antiquated and aberrant of the nuns. In Grade Nine, our Latin teacher told us solemnly, and in the hearing of the handful of Protestants and Jews whose parents believed strongly enough in a private-school education to send their daughters to our female version of Dotheboys Hall, that only baptized Catholics would escape the searing eternity of Hell.

Our Grade Ten teacher, a sweet, trembling little Chihuahua of a woman, had never taken Latin herself, and acquired dark circles under her eyes from staying up nights in an attempt to master the second-conjugation verbs before her far more enthusiastic pupils did. After that, Sisters that we never saw in any other walk of school life would come shuffling into the classroom, a copy of the textbook (paradoxically entitled *Living Latin*) clenched in a tremulous hand, to intone *"Salvete, puellae!"* in a dusty, unused voice, and then turn a literally deaf ear to the *"Salve, Soror"* that we politely chorused back.

Once, only once, when I'd reached Grade Twelve, where only the very rarefied few remained as Latin scholars, did they send us a Sister with most of her five senses intact. But she turned out to be a bloodthirsty ghoul, far more interested in recalling dismemberments she'd read about in a student's confiscated copy of *Police Gazette* than in dissecting the far less gory mysteries of "The Grinner" by Catullus.

But even as the pedagogical personnel altered year by year, *Living Latin* remained forever the same, striving, in keeping with its up-tempo, Chamber of Commerce-style name, to play up the contemporary potential of ancient Rome by using stills from Hollywood sand-and-sandal flicks as illustrations of daily Latin life.

A chapter, for example, on the various applications of the Ablative of Time might be enlivened by a shot of Jean Simmons in lipstick and a tiara trying to pass herself off as a

Roman Empress in an ablative-laden discussion with Victor Mature as a slave in just as much lipstick, but no tiara. Or a bunch of brawny Italian extras from *Quo Vadis* would stand around in gladiatorial poses to provide context for the conjugation of *"pugno, pugnare"*, "I fight".

In copies of *Living Latin* inherited from older siblings, the face of Jean Simmons had of course been embellished with ballpoint pimples, moustache, and ludicrously crossed eyes, while a leering Victor Mature inquired, in an ungrammatical balloon directed at his mouth, *"Puella, amas essere mecum in flagrante delicto?"*

Of course, in a Catholic school, Latin maintained some kind of vestigial relevance, since we girls were frequently hired out all over town to sing free-lance Requiem masses at various churches, where there always seemed to be an abundance of departed souls to commemorate, but a distinct shortage of choirs versed in Gregorian chant.

When it came to the mass, we girls knew it all, from the fervent excesses of *"Sanctus, Sanctus, Sanctus!"* to the terrifying cadences of *"Dies irae, dies illa"*, all of it, incidentally, delivered in the rolling inflections of medieval Church Latin. The day that the Latin mass was decreed obsolete was a dark one for those of us who'd laboured for years to commit to memory the precise wording of the Our Father (*"Pater noster, qui es in coelis"* . . . I can hear it yet) or the specific marching rhythms of the *Credo* (" . . . *beata Maria, semper Virgine, beato Michaeli Archangelo, beato Joanni Baptiste . . .*")

What? Latin was out, and the so-called vernacular was in? Then what had become of the Church's boast that you could go anywhere in the Catholic world, even to the reaches of darkest South Dakota, and hear the Gloria intoned in exactly the same soporific way? Suddenly we all felt exactly as the Roman Emperor must have felt the day the messenger arrived to tell him the Visigoths were overrunning the Empire.

Those of us who went on to more secular adventures in university Latin classes soon discovered that good old Church Latin was even deader than we'd expected, when it came to tweedy Protestant professors intoning "Wany, weedy, weeky", and "Weerum westis fackit", instead of the rolling Italianate cadences of our bloodthirsty nun ("Veerum vaystees fawcheet"), who may have been deficient in certain pedagogical respects, but at least knew the *real* way Latin was supposed to be pronounced.

But however we chose to inflect our Latin, and from whatever social renegades we had learned it, some thread of common purpose ran through all of us who'd persisted throughout high school and even beyond, employing that quaint, eggheaded tongue. For those of us devoid of Celtic heritage, Latin was as good a banner as Gaelic to rally behind, when we were in a mood to explore our roots. And even today, when we don't give a hoot for roots any more, ferreting out fellow Latin lovers from the ancient days of adolescence gone past is a reliable barometer for assessing prospective friends.

Latin lovers are the people who say things like *"Ars longa, vita brevis,"* when others are remarking, *"Che serà, serà."* They look askance at tea brewed in bags, wonder why anyone found it necessary to invent automatic transmission, and actually start sentences with the pronoun "one", even though one has not a drop of British blood in one's veins. Old Latin students never die, they just dote on reruns of *The Robe*, would rather bother lacing up their runners than press them closed with Velcro, cause comment in the pharmacy by asking for tooth-powder, and know how to value a light switch with buttons you can push.

Barring the availability of coffee spoons, they will measure out their lives in ounces, inches, or any unit that is not a multiple of ten. They have never found it necessary to crunch a number, access a file, or run a concept past a single soul, for they are too busy cooking oatmeal (*not* the five-minute kind), hanging up on friends whose telephones subject them to "call waiting", and scouring the town for carbon paper because on principle they refuse to require a typewriter to print out.

It is, one is well aware, a world gone by that will never come again. The leisurely sun-drenched afternoons on which we sprawled by the ball diamond at recess and chanted, *"Fuebam, fuebas, fuebat, fuebamus, fuebatis, fuebant,"* as if such things mattered, because, at the time, such things did. And scrawled on the school-washroom mirror in lipstick, *"Ego eram hic,"* because it was important that we *had* been here, even if "here" was a place in which pallid-faced nuns decreed that young Christian women did not either wear lipstick or write on washroom mirrors.

In more recent years, suddenly and inexplicably nostalgic for those bygone days of Latin ritual, I discovered a coven (and there is no other appropriate word) of retrograde Catholics, holding unsanctioned Latin masses in a catacomb-like basement meeting-room of a downtown Toronto hotel. (Since demolished, by the way – perhaps by papal decree.)

When I arrived one Sunday morning for mass – very tentatively, having not graced the inside of a Catholic church, either Latinate or otherwise, for at least fifteen years – I was astounded to see the subterranean parishioners decked out in sartorial and tonsorial styles not seen above ground since around (I mean circa) 1958.

There were little boys in H. R. Haldeman-emulating brush cuts, men in oxblood wingtips with perforations around the toe, and unsmiling women wearing – most significant of all – dowdy hats and kerchiefs. Significant, I say, because before I was allowed to take my place in one of the hotel's metal stacking-chairs, a large and demonstrably ultra-Catholic woman sternly handed me a scarf with which to cover my head in an acknowledgement of female subordination that had been diplomatically dropped from official Catholic observance, along with Latin, in the same era of sweeping reform.

Ulp, I thought, accepting my humbling headgear with gritted teeth, and slipping into a row of suppliants who faced the *back* of a renegade priest, who was defiantly offering mass pointed in a direction abandoned by the same let-it-all-hang-out regime, which had decreed, along with all the other groovy new rites, that the priest at the altar ought to look the congregation right straight in the eye.

Worst of all, the Latin I had come to hear was being

slurred and droned in an oddly familiar way that I had totally forgotten, and now recollected all too well. In the past, for most people in church, Latin had merely been the way things were, a dull ritual they didn't think much about and certainly didn't listen to. In the present, for these few fanatics, it was merely another badge of reactionary achievement, to pin on with the others.

Later on, when the interminable service had ended and I was attempting to flee, I was snagged by the severe heavy woman, who not only wanted the scarf back (she could *have* it), but also demanded to know if I planned to return next week. I told her I wasn't sure (although I *was*), and she urged me strongly to make a formal alliance with the group, since all of our earthly days were numbered, thanks to the Teamsters.

I must have betrayed more surprised curiosity than I'd intended, for she hurried on to tell me that since the Church had fallen into trendy Ecumenism, none of us had long to live. This intelligence was derived, she said, from a late-night radio broadcast by a conservative priest down in the States, whence all important religious announcements presumably came.

Gather canned goods, the priest had instructed, and hoard provisions in readiness for a union-inspired truckers' strike that was about to close down every highway in North America and lead directly on to Armageddon. The food riots were going to be many and horrible, and only the few to whom God had chosen to drop the hint about canned goods were going to survive. Perhaps, in fact, I might be interested in taking home a pamphlet telling me what exactly to stock up on, in anticipation of . . .

"No, please," I whimpered, just before I bolted. "Actually, I only came here for the Latin."

"Oh, that." And the fat woman sniffed dismissively. Clearly, Latin, unlike hoarding, was the one article of faith there was no fervour in discussing.

Years from now, I'm well aware, other younger grown-ups will reminisce about the rapturous days before New Math, before microchips in the classroom, and before laser surgery was performed on frogs in Biology class. But for those of the generation I come from and the temperament I inhabit, the world will always divide itself into Those Who Loved Latin and Those Who Did Not. It's as good a way, *pace* Caesar and the partitioning of Gaul, to divide up the world as any.

Speak Low When You Speak FM

In recent years, a lot of attention – too *much* attention, if you ask me – has been paid to the concept of personality types "A" and "B". The way the story goes, you are either a classic Type A (over-achieving, twitchy, driven to succeed) or a Type B – which means you are phlegmatic, unmotivated, and, to put it bluntly, the sort who needs to be ordered in out of the rain.

If only the whole thing were as simple as that. While it's absolutely true that there *are* two basic personality types, that "A" and "B" business is strictly for blood groups. The two *real* personality categories, subtle, complex, and essentially incompatible, can be more accurately delineated as AM and FM.

166

You have to trust me on this one. See, I've worked in radio, and I can appreciate these distinctions. In fact, it was when I made the transition from an FM program in stereo to hosting an AM radio show that I began to understand what a wide chasm I was attempting to vault.

The problem was, I spoke only FM. I was the type who referred to "a recent reissue of a fine old Angel recording", instead of "a golden oldie", as an AM announcer is required by broadcast law to say. The composers I'd mentioned on FM as "hearkening to the inspiration of a rollicksome Muse", had to become "good old boys" over on the AM dial. Indeed, my complete fluency in the AM tongue was indisputably established only when I discarded phrases like "a variegated repertoire for your audial delectation", in favour of "good-lookin' music comin' at ya".

And the linguistic distinctions go far beyond mere musical vocabulary. FM types speak of "data that can be delineated without a major assault on veracity", at the same time as native speakers of AM talk about "the straight poop".

Well, you don't have to be a genius (sorry, AMers, I mean "a brain") to perceive that the development of these separate languages stems from the need to express utterly different personalities and to embrace a myriad (i.e., a whole bunch) of opposing characteristics that go far beyond the two major frequency bands on most radios.

Not only do FM people speak FM, they lead FM lives. For example, in order to unwind at the end of a hectic day in the library stacks, a typical FMer enjoys a long bath scented with some herbal fragrance purchased on that hiking trip through the Lake District two summers ago. The AM personality, on the other hand, enjoys a vigorous shower with a loofah – one of the few foreign-sounding words he permits into his vocabulary or his life.

While the FM personality prefers to travel around town by streetcar, clutching a volume of Henry James and a paper twist full of wine-gums, the AM type still owns that Volkswagen beetle he acquired in a swap for the complete works of Alan Watts and two joints back at Berkeley, where he took a summer course one time. The beetle is named Stokely – for reasons the AMer can no longer remember.

By now, you're getting the idea, I'm sure. But just in case you aren't yet absolutely positive of what properly constitutes AM and FM, here is a quick checklist of some of the major differences:

FM	AM
alfalfa sprouts in a pita	Big Mac
pleated wool skirt in clan tartan	faded denim culottes
Alistair Cooke	Bob Barker
Abyssinian cat named Haile Selassie	bull terrier named Deputy Dawg
rambling old cottage up on Georgian Bay	Club Med
Rainer Werner Fassbinder	Steven Spielberg
Dorothy L. Sayers	Raymond Chandler
"The Birds" by Respighi	"The Byrds' Greatest Hits"
Dubonnet	Upper Canada Lager
wire whisk	blender
Pierre Trudeau	Garry Trudeau

Classifying your friends according to type is easy, of course. Those who are brisk but not boorish, somewhat American-oriented in personality, sensual, and basically comfortable with the status quo are natural AMers. Those who are retiring, convoluted, Britishy (regardless of racial inheritance), and altogether a tad twee, belong in the FM column in the ledger of life.

Things get trickier, however, when you attempt to work out which pigeonhole you yourself belong in by right. After all, who of us isn't a bit old-fashioned in some moods, fanciful and dreamy and nostalgic for seminars in English Literature? While at other moments straight-ahead, desperately modern, and so relaxed with the culture we live in that we can actually take a coolerful of beers to the beach, string up a net, and play volleyball with a bevy of suntanned companions.

We are, of course, much more complex than our easily assigned friends, and contain within us the seeds of both the AM and FM types. Roughly translated, this means we have the capacity to regard a "traditional Christmas" as one spent either with Bing Crosby or with the Early Music Consort. How these warring internal elements may be successfully resolved is, alas, material for another discussion altogether.

Gone on Dogs

If you've been wondering why your cat is particularly out of sorts lately, you haven't been looking very closely at the street, where the answer is more than obvious: Our entire society has gone completely and utterly to the dogs.

Where once the local kitsch store stood, with its inventory of cat pyjamas, cat tea-cosies, cat napkins, and cat calendars, now there is a poodle-grooming parlour. Bookstore shelves, previously reserved for cat desk-diaries, cat picturebooks, and drolly titled cat-alogues, are now given over to *Know Your German Shepherd*. Even in pet shops, the pegs once festooned with catnip mice in cello bags are today laden with rawhide bones and chewable mailmen.

What happened to the cat? Nothing. Cats, obdurate creatures that they are, are pretty much unchanged and unchangeable. The fault, therefore, is not in them, but in their stars, that they have become underlings. For what *has* changed is us – human society, and what it requires of its pets.

Time was, when we were young and footloose, our independence expressed itself perfectly through the cat. If a cat was aloof, we were aloofer – holding relationships at arm's length with ambivalent charm. If cats were fickle, we were fickler; we postponed commitment and bought second-hand – and then only when we weren't able to borrow or rent.

In fact, in those days, the only people we knew who had dogs were guys at the beach with frisbees, or else the serious sort of man who occasionally came courting in a long leather coat and replied "Indeed", no matter what the question. Absolutely everyone else had cats.

Now, of course, absolutely everyone has kids and cars and cottages and computers, and so it follows they must also have dogs. After all, why shouldn't they, when life is so encumbered already?

It sounds simple enough, and would be, if anything were simple in the world we inhabit. But the mere decision to add a dog to the entourage is only the beginning of the available choices. Indeed (as those leather-coated men of yore might say), one of the major selling-points of the dog in a society glutted with consumer options is the bewildering range of styles, sizes, fabrics, and colours he comes in.

Think about it. When choosing a cat, all that was involved was a few basic decisions like male or female, long hair or short, and spots or stripes. But selecting a dog involves looking at more than a hundred models, nervously aware all the time that whether you go for ears that are lopped or cropped, a tail that wags or wiggles, or a coat that curls or cascades, you are going to end up not only acquiring a pet, but also making an image statement about yourself and your family that would be profound, if anything succeeded by a term like "image statement" could realistically be thought of as profound.

Just by way of illustration, let's look at some of today's

more popular breeds of dogs to learn what we can about the people who might choose each one of them.

The Golden Retriever. Very high, of course, on the list of anyone who rates the Nostalgia Factor important in his life. The lovable lolloping golden retriever proclaims the 1950s in every swipe of his indiscriminate tongue and every bright glance from his steady brown Louis St. Laurent-era eyes.

A retriever family will also own a wood-panelled vehicle with four-wheel drive, at least one knitted sweater with ducks in flight on it, a Thistle pram, a complete set of the *Encyclopaedia Britannica*, and a push-style lawn-mower, because they like "that wonderful shearing sound on a summer morning".

Nostalgic types are often prosperous types too, which means the retriever family also enjoys riding lessons, vacations at the Epcot Center, and state-of-the-art orthodontics.

The West Highland White Terrier. Known as the "little white Scottie on the whiskey bottle" to those of you who are not as up on your dogs as you might be, the Westie is favoured by childless couples whose sense of gentle optimism is not as highly evolved as that of the retriever folk, or by single women who feel a cat would be an admission of having given up.

Whoever owns a West Highland White also wears cardigans, needs glasses, answers tersely on the telephone, and will choose rubber boots with thick socks over more Canadian-tailored winter footgear. As a matter of fact, there is a touch of Anglophilia about the terrier fan, who enjoys a spot of sherry, the works of Robert Graves, and garden gloves from Liberty's, and has had at least one erotic dream featuring Sheridan Morley.

Westie people are no-nonsense people, who admit to being "in a mood", but never depressed, refuse to drive when they can walk, and believe firmly that there is a job in this country for anyone who wants one.

The Borzoi. You may know this sleek, fleet giant with a head like a shoe-horn as the Russian wolfhound. By either name, he is enormous, exotic, and beloved of those who like a dog to make a statement as well as a poo when he's out for his walk. Borzoi owners absolutely detest every other animal except their own, and you won't find them down at the annual meeting of the local animal shelter, anxiously debating the proper fate of unclaimed kittens. To the Borzoi aficionado, a kitten is merely Sasha's light snack.

Fur, reptile skins, and emu feathers are preferred apparrel, and for getting around town, it's a taxi or nothing.

We're talking about night people here, avant-garde people, people beside whom David Bowie looks like a fresh-faced ad for a vitamin supplement. These are people who haven't even heard about filter-tips yet, much less lung cancer, and find their dog appealing because not only does he look hungry, he looks capable of running his lunch to earth.

The curious often ask about the difference between Borzoi people and Doberman pinscher people. Just this: Borzoi owners dress in something that matches the dog's fur. Doberman owners dress to match the harness.

The Shar-pei. "The Shar *who?*" I hear you exclaim. You know the dog I mean: the trendy, wrinkly one from China, right up there with the Australian shepherd and the Akita from Japan as the ultimate in canine conversation-pieces.

The Shar-pei owner, when quizzed about his occupation, will very often say "film producer", although that is not always strictly true. If being a film producer means drinking enormous quantities of café au lait from bowls in outdoor cafés, sending congratulatory telegrams to Oscar-winners who have never heard of you, and taking over a large table at a fashionable pasta restaurant with seven of your noisiest and drunkest friends, then the Shar-pei possessor is a film producer all right.

But when it comes to actually having produced a film, or even being on a first-name basis with those who have, the Shar-pei person will hastily duck all hard questions by taking the dog for a walk.

The dog itself, of course, looks like a Slinky toy that got stalled on a stair and all bunched up, and often the owner is hard-pressed to know at which end to attach the leash. But the pooch looks awfully good on the leather front seat of the soon-to-be-repossessed Jaguar sedan, and when accosting visiting Hollywood actresses hopeful of a quiet lunch in a hotel coffee shop, it's always nice to have the dog on hand as a conversational ice-breaker.

Otherwise, life for the Shar-pei person isn't all sweetness and sourness and Szechuan Hot and Crispy Duck. There are 7 a.m. workout classes to attend, hostile divorced spouses to try to placate with hasty phone calls from the hairdresser, hostile hairdressers to try to placate with hasty calls on the cellular carphone, and hostile cellular-carphone salesmen to placate with the same vague promises of financial satisfaction that have been palmed off on all the others.

Ultimately, as a result of monetary exigency, the Shar-pei himself will go the way of the Jaguar, the cellular carphone, and the workout classes, as just another aspect of a lifestyle that was eventually unsustainable. And of all the divestitures, the loss of the dog will hurt the most. After all, no other accoutrement of the chic, uptown, and now vanished life was wittily named Peiping Tom.

Speaking of accoutrements, the choice of a breed of dog to express the inner human self is not the only deliberation connected with canine ownership that must be considered. Just as the dog himself acts as an animate accessory to complement the other appointments of the owner's life, so too must the dog have accessories of his own to help him make a definitive statement about just whose little dog he is.

A knitted coat. It's hard for a dog not to get a laugh in one of these. However, mysteriously, a flannelette coat doesn't seem to strike the public as nearly so ridiculous, perhaps because of some positive association with thoroughbred horse racing.

In any case, a dog who feels the cold is smart to urge his owner in the direction of fabric, rather than needlework. Under *no* circumstances, however, can little rubber booties be worn with anything resembling dignity.

A chain-link collar. For some unfathomable reason, this is much more desirable as a piece of dog jewellery than a leather collar with a buckle. No one is completely sure why; possibly it's because a dog in a chain collar looks very reassuringly like a suntanned young all-American type, with a silver ID bracelet – eager, open, and full of wholesome energy. Plus, there's that extra jolly jingle of the dog-tag striking against the metal links of the collar.

A polka-dot kerchief. Now you're talking. The ultimate, the *dernier cri*, in doggy chic. *But only if you happen to be the right kind of dog!* While it's indisputable that there is no shepherd or husky or Airedale alive whose general appearance isn't enhanced by the raffish touch of an engineer's neckerchief in red or navy with white polka dots, there are certain stubby little dogs who should avoid this look at all costs. A dachshund with a neck scarf, for instance, will put one in mind of Dr. Ruth attempting to impersonate a Mexican bandit, while a Pekinese with a kerchief resembles nothing so much as a prune in a sling. Doggy discretion is advised.

As you can see, the world of canine ownership is fraught with complications you may not have considered. There will no doubt be moments when the faint-hearted will look back longingly to the comparatively straightforward Years of the Cat. But society cannot move backward, as we know, only forward. Be grateful, at least, that no mention was made here of the social implications of the cockatiel, the iguana, and the ferret. The dog has been more than enough for one day.

The Ladies' Home Companion

The one and only time I ever had a conversation with a Hollywood actress, I was impressed not so much by her burgeoning career and dazzling life as by the fact that she had a paid secretary-companion.

Well, my dear. You can keep the Malibu beach-house, the silver Porsche, and the Afghan pooch named Pucci. Just give me the paid companion. And while you're at it, see if she has eleven or so friends to come work for the eleven or so other women I know who could also use some order in their lives.

Time was, liberated women joked about needing "wives". But wife-like men turned out not to be the answer, for the simple reason that the minute a man starts behaving as solicitously as one of Hemingway's wives, a woman starts behaving like Hemingway. You know – laughing at him at Pamplona when the bullfights make him cry, bullying him in front of large groups of people for splitting his infinitives. Stuff like that.

Far better, really, to save men for romantic detail and, for those practical chores, to hire yourself a professional factotum.

Actually, I've already hired mine. Well, *hired* is too strong a word, since on my budget I can hardly afford the kid who delivers the paper. So I've done the next best thing: I've made up a paid companion.

Her name is Hildegarde (I never considered a manservant; don't ask me why) and I'd be lost without her. Hildegarde controls every aspect of my previously chaotic life from the moment I get up in the morning, without ever so much as letting me know she's doing it.

My day starts in a civilized way at about 9 a.m. when Hildegarde comes into my room with a glass of juice, coffee, a furled newspaper, and a single rose in a vase, all tastefully arranged on a tray. Then she gently rouses me by opening the drapes. (She must have bought those drapes while I was asleep, to replace the tacky blind from Canadian Tire, which has always hung crooked because I lacked the necessary working knowledge of Tagalog to read the instructions for assembly.)

Thank God I no longer need to get up at the crack of dawn to jog. Hildegarde goes jogging *for* me, and is back home in time to see to my tray. What a woman.

While I'm opening the morning's mail (which, since Hildegarde, consists entirely of cheques and fan mail), Hildegarde is either on the phone setting up the day's appointments or performing those myriad behind-the-scenes tasks that have made me a far more creditable figure in the working world.

No more Pagliacci laughs from the accountant when he sees me coming at tax time with nothing but a large brown envelope marked "Receipts, T-4s, 'n Stuff". Grown editors no longer weep openly when I submit my copy on tiny soiled sheets of floral notepaper, feverishly purchased from a dusty shelf at the local variety store because inspiration struck at 10:47 p.m. and I was out of typing-paper. Gone too are the days when, running late as usual, I'd rush from the comparative gloom of the house out into the morning sunlight, only to discover that the front of my dress was embossed with an odd spill that looked like the winning entry in a third-grader's relief-map-making project.

Best of all, Hildegarde never feels one whit demeaned by handling the mundane details of my life, and willingly gives up her weekends to service my bicycle, and mulch the roses.

Hildegarde is, in fact, by far the most satisfying fantasy of a non-sexual nature I've ever had, and I'll bet you wish *you'd* thought of her first. I mean, haven't you always craved someone to go out and buy your clothes for you, elbowing aside the skinny derisive teenagers who can't believe you mean to get into that miniskirt? Wouldn't it be terrific never to run out of stamps, pantyhose, or quarters for the washing-machine again? How would it be to have someone on tap to transcribe phone numbers into your address book from those easy-to-lose scraps of paper? Someone who also knows how to trim hair, run a word processor, and shirr eggs, whatever shirred eggs might be?

I do, however, have one eensy-weensy little criticism of life with a paid woman companion: Now that Hildegarde is on the scene, answering my phone, sharpening my pencils, sorting my records, and misting the plants, nothing – absolutely *nothing* – is standing in the way of my getting down to some serious work.

Uh-oh. Quick, Hemingway, what do I do now?

A FONDUE FAREWELL

Hands up, everyone old enough to recall fondue. Oh, come on. You remember. . . . There was the enamelled pot of vivid hue – or perhaps *your* fondue set was the classier kind in copper. In any case, you can't possibly have forgotten the little bunsen burner glowing away underneath. And those forks of tiniest tine, each handle flecked by a dot of a different color – like a marker in some absurdist gastronomic board-game – so that one could always identify one's own cube of sizzled meat or one's personal maraschino cherry luxuriating in a swamp of chocolate.

Fondue is no more. Fondue came and went more or less concomitantly – and with the same inexplicability – as the Nehru jacket. And you know something? When fondue died, something died in all of us too.

Because when we were young couples in the sixties, fondue was where it was at (along with expressions like "where it's at"). First of all, there was something sophisticated and vaguely European about all those little bottles of pricey fondue sauces you could buy. On the other hand, fondue still managed to accommodate our hippiesque urge towards informality, with its attendant ritual of sitting around the pot all night, just sizzling, dipping, and consuming.

So successful was fondue as a sort of paleface potlatch that each time a new couple got married another young couple of similar inclination could be counted upon to give a fondue set as a wedding present – just as they had been gifted with a fondue set on *their* nuptial day.

In fact, sometimes other couples got so carried away in their enthusiasm for spreading the good news about fondue that there were many of us who received more than one fondue set as a wedding gift. But that was cool too, since it opened up the possibility of an entire fondue *meal* – with one pot boiling up oil to cook the meat, another bubbling with melted cheese to dip the Franch bread bits in, and yet another full of seething chocolate wherein fruit could be immersed when the time came for dessert.

You see my point? No pretensions to *haute cuisine* in those straightforward bygone days. Nothing refined or recondite about that communal hunching over a pot of hissing oil, faces flushed from the radiated heat, partitioned fondue plates smeared like palettes with the ochres, carmines, and burnt siennas of so many daubs of sauces.

Absolutely no talent or self-expression required in the preparation or presentation of a fondue dinner. Heck, any donkey could do fondue. You could even imagine those banal and bumbling Kraft hands on the TV commercials dealing competently with the task of cutting meat, shredding bread, and mixing up homemade sauces, loosely organized around the theme of Miracle Whip.

And maybe that was the problem. Fondue was just too damn *easy*, and in the food-fetishist times we currently live in, it simply won't do anymore. It's become, in fact, a case of fon*don't*.

No, seriously, think about it. From a pinnacle of absolute chic, reached approximately fifteen years ago, fondue has descended to the depths presently occupied by such culinary risibles as frozen strawberries, the Patti-Stacker, and chip dip made from onion soup mix.

Which brings us to perhaps the most important consideration of them all: Where have all the fondue pots gone?

They can't merely have disappeared. I mean, even though those communally-oriented young couples of the sixties have turned into uptight eighties overachievers, who invite forty of their closest business associates over for a stand-up buffet of sashimi, *osso buco*, and deep-fried Brie, they must have found some practical uses for those fondue sets of yore. Of course they have.

So, where have all the fondue pots gone? Gone to flower planters, every one. Or to water dishes for the dog, or vessels to melt depilatory wax in. Or perhaps something handy for the nanny to warm up the baby's bottle.

While the fondue forks are only good now to poke a new hole in a Camp Beverly Hills belt. And the young couples who fondued so long ago have gone on to divorce, remarriage, and new meaningful relationships with their pasta-makers.

I miss the young couples that we were. I miss the cheap nights out at the campus film society, the concept of incense sticks as "atmosphere", the refrigerator in the living-room, the beaded curtain that tried and failed to establish an Indian-cotton-covered day-bed as a separate room, the late-night plans to start an alternative newspaper, the late-night arguments over a name for the alternative newspaper, the late-night decision to postpone starting an alternative newspaper until we could agree on a name. Shucks, I even miss the obligatory mandala poster on the wall.

But most of all I miss the fondue sets, and the innocent times we lived in, when food was only an excuse to get together with people you liked to talk of more important things.

One Hundred Uses
of a
Dead Relationship

Back in the fifties (before you were even *born*, right?) every women's magazine contained tips on ways to reuse everyday household items. *Family Circle*, for instance, might have step-by-step instructions on how to convert an old Javex bottle into a cunning piggy-bank. *Chatelaine* was likely to explain how Crisco tins might be painted and decal-ed and turned into attractive sugar canisters. Even *Harper's Bazaar* was not above a little thrifty retooling. "Why don't you rinse your blonde child's hair in dead champagne," ran the rhetorical demand, "to keep it gold, as they do in France?" Hey, now why didn't I think of that?

Then came the sixties (which are okay to remember, as long as it's dimly) and recycling was the rage. Which simply meant the Javex-bottle idea applied on a global level and rechristened Ecology.

Now, in the 1980s, we're ready for a further development of the recycling concept. Relationships. After all, if there are a hundred uses of a dead cat, there must be at least as many ways to recycle a dead love affair. Especially when you consider the current high turnover in this area, at the same time as you are considering the following:

Old boyfriends, many women report, make excellent cat-sitters. For one thing, old boyfriends can be counted upon to know in intimate and often mind-numbing detail all of your cat's likes, dislikes, and personal peculiarities. After all, this was the kind of stuff they were forced to take an avid interest in when your relationship was hot. Now that it's not, all that accumulated knowledge has practical applications.

For another thing – and this is key – old boyfriends often have enough residual guilt about the way the relationship ended to make them easily exploitable on short notice. Which means that not only can a former flame be pressed into cat-sitting service whenever a sudden business trip calls you out of town, he won't even expect to be reimbursed for the catfood and litter he had to purchase in your absence.

And there's more good news. Even if you aren't a pet owner, you can still find many ways to come out of a dead relationship a winner. For instance, old boyfriends have been documented as the world's leading source of novelty sleepwear for women. This, however, is not merely a reference to all those filmy negligées and cute camisoles they bought for you back in the saccharine days when your anniversaries were reckoned on a weekly basis. As any woman knows, the *real* score in the naughty-nightie department has got to be an old Led Zeppelin T-shirt, size X-Large. And while the permanent acquisition of his Pierre Cardin près-du-corps body shirt in a nice Tattersall check may not totally compensate for the loss of the man, it can certainly go a long way toward easing the pain.

Perhaps best of all in the realm of simple recycling (especially if you're into recurrent motifs of death, resurrection, and life eternal) is the way old boyfriends give rise to new platonic friendships. Not necessarily with *him*. Although old lovers may in certain instances sea-change into friends, don't count on it. It's likely that his greatest future value will always be as a cat-sitter and as a source of outsize shirts.

But *through* him you will get to meet all his other old girl-friends – witty and wonderful women who, like you, were bright enough to bail out when the going got rough. (That, at least, is the way you will tell it to each other over smart drinks and a little salad when all the other former flamettes discover you've joined their ranks and ask you out, in order to determine exactly how it was you and he broke up.)

Pondering Where It All Went Wrong is, however, not something that can be dispatched in a single evening out with the girls. Nor should you labour under some mistaken illusion that the sooner you get over him, the better. Not at all. Because if the dead relationship has one primary and all-encompassing use, it is as a foundation upon which to build a sturdy structure of mature self-analysis.

Pop-sociology books recognize this principle. Indeed, pop-sociology-book authors are the world's most productive utilizers of dead relationships. Not their own, though. Yours.

Virtually any pop-sociology book with a colon somewhere in its title can be counted upon to supply endless examples of failed relationships much like your own, and to perform autopsies on them, in an attempt to determine the various causes of death. From thence, it is an easy step to formulating a plausible social theory to explain How It All Went Wrong.

Not that there's any reason to relinquish the field of dead-relationship analysis to the so-called experts. After all, by this point in your troubled history, you've had easily as many old boyfriends as anybody else. Possibly more. In fact, you may well be in the quintessentially 1980s situation of having broken up with more men *than you've actually gone out with*. Or perhaps it just feels that way.

In any case, you have every right to forgo pensive bedtime perusal of any of the current crop of pop-sociology books in favour of some theory-formulating of your very own. If theory-formulating and dead-relationship analysis are brand new to you, however, you may find it advisable to first condition your mind to the task with some preliminary mental calisthenics.

One simple beginning exercise is to think back over the record collection of your most recent dead relationship, and to ask yourself if his musical tastes contained any hints of the emotional problems that cropped up farther down the road. A man, for example, who attempted to turn you on to his collection of Carpathian zither classics on the first date was probably a poor relationship risk right from the kickoff. Or if such glib put-her-in-the-mood standbys as Julio Iglesias and Rachmaninoff's First Piano Concerto came too readily to hand, you should have sensed he was just painting by numbers.

More important, try to recollect if any of his perennial favourites belong on the proscribed list of Records to Beware Of. This, in case you didn't know, is a compilation of familiar discs ranging from the contemporary to the classical, favoured by men who evince qualities of self-pity, remoteness, and brooding solipsism traditionally associated with Men Who Have Nothing to Give.

Did his tastes run heavily to the gravelly grumblings of Tom Waits? Was he too deeply into the more sombre offerings of Wagner? Or did he gravitate toward world-weary titles like *Running on Empty* and *Solitary Man*? Ah, well, then, no wonder your relationship with this selfish introvert died.

Equally unpromising is the crumhorn enthusiast or the Celtic Revival nut, generally as effetely precious in his personal relationships as in his auditory habits.

But if there was an unbridled enthusiasm for the works of Ralph Vaughan Williams, or unqualified approval for "Heart Like a Wheel", or a positive attitude toward the smart-assed wit of K. D. Lang . . . then you had a happy, wholesome, and well-adjusted gem on your hands, and only a blundering idiot could have let him slip away.

Unless, of course, you're *glad* he's gone, which is, most assuredly, your right. After all, mere generosity of spirit and even temper in a man are not enough in themselves to keep a relationship alive, and he may have had a hundred quirky little tastes and habits that eventually drove you around the bend. No analysis of a defunct relationship can be considered complete without a thorough re-evaluation of those tastes and habits, in order to determine which of them has remained with you, even though the man who inspired them has not. Again, a simple exercise is the best way to begin.

Ask yourself a basic question: How am I different now from the person who met _____ (fill in the blank) way back when? Be prepared to be frank with yourself here, and to face up to some pretty unpleasant truths. Perhaps your old boyfriend has left you with a permanent addiction to the novels of Ross MacDonald, even though you know in your heart that you'd really feel far more fulfilled with a volume of Alice Munro by your bed.

This on top of the fact that *previous* old boyfriends have already left you with some pretty ugly psychic scars. For example, you are still guiltily devoted to Fluffernutters (nauseating sandwiches made of white bread, peanut butter, and marshmallow topping) all because of a brief alliance with a draft-resister back in the summer of 1972, when the entire world, it seemed, lived in communal houses with a copy of the Desiderata tacked up in the john.

Later, things only got worse. You can no longer remember the name of the cute, Archie-faced lawyer who chatted you up in the parking lot of Loblaws and then phoned you for six months before you'd consent to go out with him. But you still remember to tune in to the Bugs Bunny–Road Runner Hour he so passionately championed, and you never fail to think of him when you do.

Which is, at least, a far cheaper dependency than your continued craving for Vita Bath, first introduced to you by your old fiancé, who left a ring in the tub and didn't even get around to getting the engagement ring sized properly before requesting it back.

But, making every effort to be fair about this, you do have to admit some positive habits have outlasted the relationships they sprang from. Sure they have. Didn't that nice high school teacher from Calgary show you the quick way to reckon a tip of 15 per cent? Aren't you forever indebted to the Club Med find who was the first man to notice how stunning you looked in mauve, *and* showed you how to whistle through a blade of grass? And what about that long-lost love who introduced you to *Two for the Road*, the best movie in the entire history of the cinema? The relationship, unlike the movie, may have ended badly, but at least the movie, unlike the man, still turns up unexpectedly late at night when you're cruising TV channels.

Of course, at a certain point, dead-relationship analysis runs the risk of devolving into mere navel-gazing, unless there is a larger philosophical principle at work. This is why it's important, finally, to get beyond mere nostalgia and come up with mind-expanding applications for the experiences – both good and bad – that you've undergone.

On this level, perhaps the best that can be said for dead relationships is that they reassure us that we've suffered. Evidence of suffering not only helps us delude others that we are mature, it also gives us a sense of identification with all of the world's confused and abused. This in turn enables us to nod with solemn understanding during the more anguished speeches in the plays of Anton Chekhov, and to write "Too true" in the margins of Anaïs Nin's diaries.

There are also the *social* advantages of a tortured past to consider. What would lunch with other women be if you couldn't hold up your end when the gruesome stories are trotted out and swapped? Your friend Marlene is threatening to dominate the conversation with her harrowing account of Ralph-the-String-Saver and how he's told Marlene that the sight of her in shorts caused him to associate productively to the word "tapioca" in his therapy session.

Isn't it nice to know that this is a moment at which you can bring the focus of attention smartly back to yourself, where it belongs, by confiding the terrible details of the demise of *your* most recent dead relationship, barely cold on the slab?

"I couldn't believe what we were arguing about. Whether Citizen Kane drops the snow-shaker thing before or *after* he says 'Rosebud'. Can you believe that? Two educated grown-ups with a combined income of one hundred and twenty thousand dollars a year, and we're breaking up over the final four seconds of an old movie? The next thing I know, he's storming through the apartment, gathering up the espresso-maker, his ankle weights, and the Glen Loates books, and heading for the door. I can't even remember if he told me to drop dead before or *after* he slammed it.'

"That's nothing," your friend Mimi will console you at this point. "Lennie and I broke up over whether the red roses went with the House of Lancaster or the House of York."

Mimi's brand of one-upwomanship is to be expected when dead relationships are under discussion. As you travel life's highway, wading deeper and deeper through the broken crockery of ruptured romances, the only thing that may eventually keep you going is the smug assurance that you're living life closer to the edge of raw visceral experience than anybody you know.

If Maribeth has been disappointed by seventeen guys in the past year, you've failed to find happiness with twenty. If Melissa's man was insensitive enough to bow out in the midst of her plantar-wart trauma, how does that stack up against *your* back-number, who timed the break-up to occur on the same day you lost your job and the budgie got sick? And so on and so on.

But when all is said and done, all the dead relationships in the world will do little for your social standing unless you are prepared to turn yourself into a prognosticator, willing and able to make amatory predictions for your woman friends at the drop of a hat. After all, if there's one thing that's more fun than getting the gang together to mourn the demise of yet another modern union, it's getting together with one very close friend to hear all about the new man she's just met. Think how your value as a confidante will be enhanced if you are able, on the basis of seemingly trivial evidence, to give her firm odds on her relationship's chances for future survival.

Getting the hang of punditry isn't as difficult as you might think. For one thing, other women's lives are always simpler than your own, and therefore easier to figure. For another thing, other women's *men* are easier to figure too, and once you know what to look for, coming up with snap judgments should pose no problem at all.

Basically, other women's men divide themselves into three main categories: the Good, the Bad, and the Iffy. Within these categories are specific characteristics which can provide accurate clues as to the Relationship Potential (known in the trade as the R.P.) of the man in question.

One surefire sign of a Good man is his immediate willingness to lend his car, even before the relationship is well under way. A man who lets others into his car will also allow free-and-easy access to his books, his time, his thoughts, and, eventually, even his old shirts – which, as previously stated, count for a lot, regardless of what else is going on in the relationship.

The Bad man, on the other hand, not only treats requests for his car keys as though he were being asked for an on-the-spot kidney donation, he can also be identified by his tendency to complain bitterly and often about getting old.

Ask the woman friend who's taken up with a new man how frequently he can be found sighing tragically into the mirror about his thinning hair. Does he dwell on his back problems? Refuse to wear his glasses in a restaurant, preferring to frown at the menu at arm's length, with an expression that suggests a plot to poison him might be hidden somewhere in the list of entrées?

If she answers "yes" to any of the above, it's your duty to inform her that her new relationship is already in trouble. Age-obsessed guys are unhappy guys who stopped reaching out the day they stopped reaching their toes.

Other high-risk indications of a Bad man include daily phone conversations with his ex-wife, which says less about the concept of creative divorce than it does about his inability to get on with his life. Then there's the man who says, "I'll call you. . . . Or you call me." Principles of equality notwithstanding, experience teaches us that keeping things loose very soon degenerates into keeping things vague. Finally, all women should be on their guard against any man who says, "No, not in that drawer. That's the *green* twist-tie drawer."

Good men have dogs, but order them to leave the room during love-making. Good men enjoy their jobs and, what is more, enjoy their girlfriends' jobs too. Most important, Good men show no inclination in the world to talk about computers, unless it's to ask a woman to explain how the damn thing works.

Meanwhile, in the Iffy category falls the man who checks out well in the car-lending and young-at-heart departments, but who keeps a bewildering array of fresh toothbrushes, new combs, and even boxes of tampons on hand in his bachelor medicine chest. Such a comprehensive pharmaceutical stock may argue for a considerate nature, but there's something premeditated about a man who maintains a supply of packaged terry robes, and is able to produce one in just your friend's size and colour the morning after their first night together.

Iffy men (wouldn't you know it) are the ones in greatest supply, and you will have to show the skill of an entrail reader if you expect to help your best friend assess the one she's landed. The fact that he gives back-massages is Good, although it *might* be Bad if she gets the feeling that all backs are the same to him in the dark. A willingness to be talkative in bed is something he shares with a Good man, unless what he talks about is treasury bills.

And what to make of the R.P. of a man who remembers to send your friend flowers on anniversaries – but it's the anniversary of the Canadian hockey team's victory over the Soviets?

In the end, no matter how you choose to participate in the wonderful world of dead relationships – whether as a recycler, a philosopher, or a pundit – there is one cardinal consideration that overrides all the others: *A dead relationship is better than no relationship at all.* Especially when you recollect that we are living in an era in which, very often, these two options represent the entire spectrum of choice in the matter.

And, of course, it's important to keep busy, while waiting for the next living relationship to come along. For instance, you might consider getting together with some of the girls this weekend, to have bags of fun turning old Javex bottles into cunning piggy-banks.

THE ROOMIE MILL

Over a second drink late at night, Sam confides that living with Edna is not exactly living up to expectation.

"Before she moved in," Sam says dolefully, "I thought it was going to be the perfect set-up. I mean, who could be more fun to live with than good old Edna? Well, I'll tell you who: Madame Defarge, Dr. Crippen, or any member of the Dalton Gang, to name a few. Edna signed away her sense of humour the day she signed that lease."

Just for the sake of clarification, I should point out a couple of things. First of all, Sam is not a man; nor is Edna her lover. I'm afraid it's more complicated than that. Edna is Sam's roommate, and thereby hangs a tale of the eighties.

"Initially," sighs Sam, signalling the waiter to bring her

191

yet another vod-and-ton, "Edna looked like the obvious solution to my problem. When Bernie moved out, he left me with nothing but my memories, notices from MasterCharge that read like hate mail, and an apartment that costs as much to heat as Windsor Castle.

"Plus, I was lonely. Who wants to go back to living alone any more? Living alone went out with beanbag chairs and cookiegrams."

To a certain extent, Sam is right. Living alone *is* out of vogue at the moment. Nor, come to think of it, can I remember the last time anyone except the cat voluntarily sat in my beanbag chair. However, I take the news about cookiegrams somewhat harder, since I have sent one this very afternoon to a man who took my fancy in a cashier line-up at the liquor store. The cookie is in the shape of a snake, and the icing caption reads, "Be My Boa." I think it rather clever, myself.

Yet in spite of the fact that, in greater and greater numbers, women are turning to each other as more logical (and perhaps even more permanent) roommates than men, I can't help feeling Sam should have foreseen some of the problems inherent in living with another woman.

For one thing, I roomed with Sam myself for a time, back in college, and I have to tell you it was no picnic. Or, rather, it was too *much* of a picnic, involving as it did lots of plastic forks and knives – because Sam could never remember when it was her turn to do the dishes – and a continual invasion of ants and other insects occasioned by Sam's inattention to details like vacuuming.

She hasn't changed much over the years, either. In fact, I suspect one of the reasons Bernie finally bailed out was that he got tired of finding Sam's false eyelashes in his tie-clip box because she couldn't think of where else to put them. Then again, perhaps the final straw was having to deal with the blobs of wax that clogged the drain whenever Sam decided to take a long bath by candlelight.

I can just imagine what effect all of this would have on a naturally tidy woman like Edna. As it happens, I am intimately acquainted with Edna's orderly ways, since I once (only once) shared a room with her on vacation. For one thing, you have to be wary of someone who irons her bathing suit. And I thought it unnecessary for Edna to carry her own bottled water into the hotel dining-room. These are the sorts of little quirks, harmless in themselves, that gradually add up to disaster – particularly when it's two *women* who are attempting to share the space.

"She won't let me make one single decision," Sam moans. "I bring home a chicken, put it in the fridge, and she's got it breaded and fried before I can turn around."

"Sam, you said it yourself. You don't want to go back to living alone."

She throws me a look that reproaches me for my lack of understanding, and I recall guiltily how crazy Edna drove me on that vacation. Then I come to my senses and remember how Sam's sloppiness undermined my final year in college. Nobody's at fault here. Sam and Edna are just a bad match.

And yet from every point of view – economic, emotional, and practical – doesn't learning to cohabit with other women make supremely good sense in a world where conventional living arrangements have become the unconventional exception?

"Sure it makes sense," Sam concedes. "Edna and I have to find a way to ease the tension. Which is where you come in."

"Me? What has this got to do with me?"

Sam gives me her most winning smile, and even bats her false eyelashes a little. "You keeping saying how sick you are of living in an apartment the size of a footlocker. My God, there's an entire *wing* in my place that's never been opened! And if Edna and I just had a buffer between us . . . ."

Sam and Edna and I, all sharing Sam's apartment together. I feel the world lurch slightly and begin to go black.

"I don't know," I mumble, wetting my lips nervously. "I'll have to give that some serious thought."

Sure, I'll give it some serious thought. Some day. Right after I've given away the beanbag chair and stopped impulsively sending cookiegrams to men in liquor store line-ups. Some day. But, please God, not quite yet.

An Account of the Yuppie Wars

It is only recently that the full impact of the bitter so-called Yuppie Wars of the late 1980s has begun to be understood. And even in the wake of understanding, there are still vast areas of ignorance surrounding the issues that inspired the Yuppies and their sworn foes the Huppies (past participle of Hippie) to clash.

What *is* clear, however, is that the battle began, not over conflicting shoe styles, as was originally believed, but over something far more basic. Food.

Of the Yuppies' culinary habits, much has already been written. While theirs was an acquisitive and hedonistic philosophy best summarized by the phrase "It's alimentary, my dear Watson," the Huppies' gustatory practices have been less well documented by social historians.

Between the 1960s, for example – when, as Hippies, this largely nomadic tribe subsisted on a diet of frozen yogurt, tahini-and-hashish sandwiches, and Fiddle-Faddle – and the 1980s, by which time they'd aged into Huppies, there is a blank space of a decade, during which it's unclear whether these people ate at all. Meatless tacos washed down with quarts of B.C. cider made an appearance some time in the seventies, but all we really know for sure is that it was in the late eighties that the battle lines between hot submarine and *haute cuisine* were clearly drawn.

The Yuppies came armed with enough *crème anglaise* to sink a battleship and sophisticated armaments like double-chocolate mousse cake soaked in Poire William, to tangle with a ragtag Huppie army led by an old communard known as the Dessert Rat. This was a commander out of touch with the times who still believed that war could be waged effectively with such antiquated weaponry as Duncan Hines Devil's Food cake dolled up with a few miniature marshmallows.

On other fronts, there were the legendary Clothes *Kriegs*, spectacular aerial battles in which silk *disegnatore* suits, fresh from management consultations at the bar of the Hong Kong Hilton, dog-fought it out with corduroy classics that had seen long service in bargaining sessions between high school English teachers and a recalcitrant Board.

But, finally and irrevocably, it all came down – as indeed most things in this world inevitably must – to a difference in vocabulary. While the Yuppies spoke of "getting that lunch thing happening," the antediluvian Huppie-types were still making fatuous plans to "haul out the Rumoli board and split a pizza, whaddaya say?"

The Yuppies referred with clear-eyed precision to "possibilities that might eventuate," while their disorganized contemporaries over in the Huppie camp still wanted to "leave it loose, okay, and see what shakes down?"

We will not devote too much attention here to the Car Wars, in which rusted-out Wagoneers attempted to take on battalions of silver Mercedes sedans, which, as one dismayed Huppie put it, came rolling up over the hill like "an army, man, of pewter bedpans!"

Perhaps more significant to document is the fact that the

Yuppies refreshed themselves at the front with foaming cappuccino, drunk from cups emblazoned with mordant observations like "Life Is Hard and Then You Die." Over in the Huppie tents, meanwhile, Chase and Sanborn (remember *them?*) was still being brewed up in a Pyrex perc, to be poured into faded mugs hazily declaring, "Jan 20 to Feb 18: Aquarius. Your age is dawning. Lucky number: Six."

Who was the ultimate victor in this cruellest and most cataclysmic of all bloodless human wars is left to you to deduce. Certainly the evidence proffered by the world in which we all now live makes clear which of these two cultures prevailed.

There will be those among you, however, who will feel yourselves experiencing twinges of furtive loyalty to the Huppies still. You will think of them, well-intentioned in Hush Puppies instead of Topsiders, on their way to a revue cinema instead of the VCR rental store, disarmingly direct with a bag of licorice all-sorts in hand instead of a beribboned box from the Belgian chocolate shop.

You may even notice alarming tendencies in yourself that you cannot explain. A wilful desire to purchase LPs when all around you are snapping up compact discs? An unaccountable temptation to throw a chili-and-sangria party instead of hiring that squad of little white-coated men to invade your backyard with their vats of wine coolers and acres of fresh-grilled salmon? Even, God forbid, the irresistible urge to jettison racquet-ball for one noonhour at least, in favour of a game of Hearts.

If so, please believe you are not alone. There is, we can only fervently hope, still a little Huppie left in everyone.

Acknowledgements

The author wishes to thank: The staff of CBC Radio's *Dayshift* for their tolerant support of her moonlighting on this book while she also hosted the show; *The Toronto Star*, for inspiring her with a weekly deadline that served to frighten work from her; Doug Gibson, for his interest in and editing of this collection; and The Canada Council, whose support was not needed for this project, but whose help and encouragement have been generously available in the past.

A number of the essays in this book have previously appeared in *The Toronto Star* and *City Woman* magazine, although some in different forms. "The Schleppy Woman's Guide to Money Management" appeared in the *Royal Bank Reporter*. The short play *Roses Are Red* was originally broadcast (in a slightly different form) on CBC Radio's *State of the Arts*, and "Stephanie Leacock" was published, in markedly different form, in a collection of critical essays, *Stephen Leacock: A Reappraisal*, edited by David Staines and published by the University of Ottawa Press.

‖DOUGLAS GIBSON BOOKS‖

PUBLISHED BY McCLELLAND AND STEWART

Other Titles

THE PROGRESS OF LOVE *by* Alice Munro

"Probably the best collection of stories — the most confident and, at the same time, the most adventurous — ever written by a Canadian."

David Macfarlane, *Saturday Night*   *Fiction 6 × 9 320 pages, hardcover*

FOUR DAYS OF COURAGE   The Untold Story of the Fall of Marcos *by* Bryan Johnson

"What may well be the best book on the Ferdinand Marcos-Corazon Aquino election campaign and on the 'People Power' that toppled a tyrant. . . ."
New York Times

Politics/Journalism 6 × 9 284 pages, map and photographs, hardcover

THE RADIANT WAY *by* Margaret Drabble

"Margaret Drabble's *The Radiant Way* does for Thatcher's England what *Middlemarch* did for Victorian England . . . Essential reading!"

Margaret Atwood   *Fiction 6 × 9 400 pages, hardcover*

DANCING ON THE SHORE   A Celebration of Life at Annapolis Basin *by* Harold Horwood *Foreword by* Farley Mowat

"Rampant with ideas about the nature of life and the universe, this book could well make Harold Horwood's Annapolis Basin another Walden Pond."
Fred Bodsworth

Nature/Ecology 5½ × 8½ 208 pages, 16 wood engravings, hardcover

NO KIDDING   Inside the World of Teenage Girls *by* Myrna Kostash

Every parent should read this frank, informative look at life among Canadian teenage girls today.

Women/Journalism 6 × 9 320 pages, notes, hardcover

THE LIFE OF A RIVER *by* Andy Russell

The affecting history of a river from the ice age, through Blackfoot times and white settlement, all the way to its planned destruction.

History/Ecology 6 × 9 208 pages, hardcover

THE HONORARY PATRON   A Novel *by* Jack Hodgins

The Governor General's Award winning author presents his first novel since 1979 — a triumphant mixture of comedy and wisdom.

Fiction 6 × 9 336 pages, hardcover

PADDLE TO THE AMAZON   The Ultimate 12,000-Mile Canoe Adventure *by* Don Starkell, *edited by* Charles Wilkins

The astonishing, terrifying journal of a father and son's canoe voyage from Winnipeg to the mouth of the Amazon.

Travel/Adventure 6 × 9 320 pages, illustrations and maps, hardcover

THE INSIDERS   Government, Business, and the Lobbyists *by* John Sawatsky

The author who got the Mounties to talk now reveals the intriguing secret world of Ottawa's lobbyists, from Pearson's days up to the present.

Politics/Business 6 × 9 320 pages, illustrations, hardcover